MULTIPLE VOICES

FOR ETHNICALLY DIVERSE EXCEPTIONAL LEARNERS

1997

BRIDGIE ALEXIS FORD
EDITOR

DDEL

A PUBLICATION OF THE
DIVISION FOR CULTURALLY AND
LINGUISTICALLY DIVERSE
EXCEPTIONAL LEARNERS

PUBLISHED BY THE COUNCIL FOR EXCEPTIONAL CHILDREN

Cover design and artwork by Corinne Elworth, Asterisk Group Inc. Original artwork for quilt piece by Marilyn Johnson, President, CEC-DDEL.

Library of Congress Catalog Card Number: 97-66899

ISBN 0-86586-295-8

A Publication of The Division for Culturally and Linguistically Diverse Exceptional Learners, a division of The Council for Exceptional Children.

Copyright 1997 by The Council for Exceptional Children, 1920 Association Drive, Reston, Virginia 20191-1589.

Stock No. D5217

Printed in the United States of America.

10 9 8 7 6 5 4 3 2 1

CONTENTS

VOLUME 2, NUMBER 1, JUNE 1997

Preview

BRIDGIE ALEXIS FORD

Editor, Multiple Voices

This year, 1997, marks the 75th anniversary of The Council for Exceptional Children (CEC). In celebration of this special occasion, a commemorative quilt containing a block reflecting each of CEC's Divisions is being constructed. The cover design on this issue of *Multiple Voices* is a replication of DDEL's quilt block. The different motifs and fabrics on each of the four hands represent the various ethnic groups of professionals working together to promote effective educational services for culturally and linguistically diverse exceptional children and their families. DDEL is a young Division within CEC; however, our members' activities span over a period of 25 years.

While we celebrate CEC's 75th anniversary, we do so with the knowledge that our children and youth are still confronted with multidimensional problems that warrant multidimensional solutions. These problems include (a) overrepresentation of culturally and linguistically diverse (CLD) youth in remedial or special education classes and underrepresentation in programming for the gifted and talented, (b) inadequate preparation of school personnel to plan and deliver effective educational services for these youth and their families, (c) biased assessment measures for identification purposes, and (d) limited involvement of CLD parents and their communities as empowered partners with the schools.

In *Multiple Voices,* DDEL publishes articles that address the paradigms, research, policies, and daily school practices that tend to either reduce or perpetuate inequities in educational opportunities for CLD individuals with disabilities and/or gifts and talents. This issue begins with an article delineating strategies to help maximize the academic skills of CLD students with behavior disorders. The second article discusses the urgent need for professionals from ethnic minority groups to write for publication.

Next are two articles that outline successful classroom intervention techniques. One describes problems and remedial activities used with an Asian-American student with a disability, and the other provides a glimpse inside the classroom of a group of African-American students with gifts and talents. The "In the Oral Tradition" section interviews three Native American professionals about critical educational issues and possible solutions to problems confronting Native American students. These articles will be helpful in providing general and special educators with tools to make sound decisions about high-quality educational programming for youth from culturally and linguistically diverse backgrounds. We believe that collaborative and consultative efforts will assist all of us in making functional goal-directed decisions as we approach the 21st century.

ACKNOWLEDGMENTS

On behalf of DDEL, I congratulate the authors of the articles in this issue of *Multiple Voices* and invite submission of manuscripts for the forthcoming issues. I thank the associate editors and Editorial Board members for their continuous commitment to quality and willingness to provide detailed, constructive critiques of the manuscripts to aid authors in their revisions, resubmissions, or reconceptualizations of their work.

Associate Editors

Bob Algozzine

Alfredo Artiles

Helen Bessent Byrd

Festus E. Obiakor

MULTIPLE VOICES MANUSCRIPT GUIDELINES

Manuscripts focusing on effective classroom/postsecondary practices, assessment, family/community empowerment techniques, research, material or test reviews, recruitment, and other issues pertaining to culturally and linguistically diverse exceptional populations are welcomed. Teachers are especially encouraged to submit work about proven practices for students with disabilities and/or those with gifts and talents. Only manuscripts not previously published and not being considered for publication may be submitted. Receipt of manuscript will be acknowledged and the manuscript will undergo a blind peer review. The author(s) must submit four copies to: Dr. Bridgie Alexis Ford, Editor, Department of Counseling and Special Education, The University of Akron, Akron, OH 44325-5007, (330) 972-6734, e-mail: alexis2@uakron.edu. The manuscript must conform to APA style (4th ed.) and not exceed 20 pages.

Developing a Multicultural and Student-Centered Educational Environment for Students with Serious Emotional Disturbances

BRIAN KAI YUNG TAM
Kean College

RALPH GARDNER, III
The Ohio State University

ABSTRACT: *By the year 2000, one third of the students in American schools will come from culturally and linguistically diverse backgrounds (Grossman, 1995). Finding the most effective method to educate a diverse population is becoming increasingly important. The burgeoning number of children from diverse ethnic backgrounds will likely further increase the disproportionate number of individuals from diverse cultural and linguistic groups who are identified with serious emotional disturbances (SED) (National Mental Health Association, 1993). This article focuses on the use of a multicultural and student-centered pedagogy and curriculum for students with SED. Embedded in the discussion are strategies (e.g., cooperative learning, peer tutoring, and three "low-tech" strategies) for educators to impact the performance of students with SED.*

American educators are facing a changing student population. There is a growing number of students who come from culturally and linguistically diverse backgrounds. In fact, by the year 2000 a third of the students in schools across the nation will be from minority families (Grossman, 1995). This change is expected to continue into the next century, when it is projected that over 40% of the school-age population will consist of students of color (Cheng, Ima, & Labovitz, 1994; Pallas, Natriella, & McDill, 1989). What are the implications of this change in demographics for special education? If current trends continue, the burgeoning number of children from culturally and linguistically diverse backgrounds will increase the already disproportionate number of individuals from diverse ethnic groups who are identified as having special needs.

Students from diverse cultural backgrounds, particularly African Americans, are disproportionately referred for behavior and learning problems (Anderson & Webb-Johnson, 1995; Council for Children with Behavior Disorders, 1989; Sugai & Maheady, 1988). Nationwide, African Americans make up 16% of the public school population but 28% of all children in special education (The Council for Exceptional Children, 1994). African Americans are also overrepresented in the category of students with serious emotional disturbances (SED) (National Mental Health Association, 1993). Students with SED generally earn lower grades and drop out at higher rates (56%) than both their typical peers and students with other disabilities (Osher, Osher, & Smith, 1994). One reason for this dismal academic record is that far too many of the classrooms for students with SED emphasize behavior management almost to the exclusion of academics (Knitzer, Steinberg, & Flesch, 1990). The lack of focus on academic performance in these classrooms may further exacerbate the academic performance gap between students with SED and their typically developing peers (Heward, 1996). An immediate consequence of this lack of emphasis on academics for students with SED is a diminished possibility of successful inclusion in general education classrooms. In fact, of all the mild disability categories, students with SED are the least likely to be placed in a general education classroom (Walker & Bullis, 1991).

Effective academic instruction is essential for students with SED in order to improve their chances for school success. Another reason for insisting on high-quality academic instruction in the SED classroom is the positive effect it may have on the social behavior of students (Gardner, 1990). Both Bullara (1994) and Hamilton (1991) found that guided notes not only improved the academic performance of secondary students with SED during social studies, but also had a positive impact on students' classroom social behavior. This replicates the effect seen in previous studies with diverse populations wherein increased active student responding to instructional stimuli was found to be positively related to appropriate social behavior (Ayllon & Roberts, 1974; Broughton & Laltey, 1978; McKenzie & Henry, 1979). Furthermore, efficacious instruction of academics increases the likelihood that students with SED will experience success in the classroom and provides an opportunity for these students to narrow the academic gap between them and their typical peers. Educators of students with SED must be concerned not only with instructional delivery, but also with the relevance of the curriculum to the learners.

Students from different cultural and linguistic groups are less likely to have information presented to them in a familiar way in their classrooms than are their European-American middle-class counterparts (Kunjufu, 1989; Midgette, 1995). Clarke and colleagues (1995)

made curriculum modifications to better match the interests of four students with SED while maintaining the integrity of the instructional objectives and found that the students' academic and social behaviors improved. Building on students' interests can play an important role in enhancing the learning process. Placing the instructional information in a context that is familiar to the student should increase the probability that the student will focus on the appropriate instructional stimulus. The use of culturally sensitive instructional information may be especially important for students with SED, given their academic needs, their propensity to be disruptive, and the overrepresentation in this category of learners from culturally and linguistically diverse backgrounds.

Determining specific pedagogical strategies for delivering a culturally sensitive curriculum is also critical in the educational process. Researchers have found that one of the most important factors affecting student achievement is the extent to which students are actively engaged during the instructional presentation (Gardner, Heward, & Grossi, 1994; Greenwood, Delquadri, & Hall, 1984; Roshenshine & Berliner, 1978). There is a growing body of literature demonstrating the functional relationship between increased active student responding and improved academic performance of students from various populations (e.g., students with specific learning disabilities, those with developmental disabilities, at-risk students, typically achieving students) (Heward, 1994). Students with SED, particularly those from culturally and linguistically diverse backgrounds, however, have not generally been a part of this research in improving academic performance. This article examines cultural and linguistic diversity of the school population with regard to students with SED and suggests several instructional strategies, coupled with a multicultural curriculum, that might improve the academic achievement of these students. This is in harmony with the National SED Agenda (U.S. Department of Education, 1994), which, as part of its seven-pronged strategy, places an emphasis on both improving the academic performance of students with SED and increasing educators' responsiveness to the race, culture, gender, and socioeconomic status of learners.

THE IMPORTANCE OF A MULTICULTURAL CURRICULUM

The examination of curricular needs for students from diverse cultural backgrounds is an important step in the education process (Franklin, 1992). Williams (1989) referred to a curriculum as the "processes used to plan, implement, and evaluate learning activities, or cumulatively, to encompass all the educational activities undertaken in a classroom. More narrowly, curriculum may refer to one stream of those activities (often representing a particular subject such as math, or language arts), which is presented in combination with other streams" (p. 82). The curriculum of a school should reflect the diversity of the school's population, should include a core body of knowledge that takes into account the students' various cultural backgrounds (Wyman, 1993), and should not focus solely on one culture to the exclusion of others (Bieger, 1996). The similarities of different ethnic groups should also be reflected in the curriculum (Barry, 1990; Hilliard, 1995). A small number or even the absence of students with culturally and linguistically diverse backgrounds in a school, however, should not eliminate the use of multicultural materials (Baker, Browdy, Beecher & Ho, 1977; Dean, Salend, & Taylor, 1993). Multicultural materials can provide students with crucial and accurate information to establish a positive attitude toward themselves and other ethnic groups.

Historically, the Eurocentric curriculum used in American schools has given a limited picture of individuals from culturally and linguistically diverse backgrounds and their contributions to this country (Scarcella, 1990). People of color frequently find themselves underrepresented in the more valued areas of society (e.g., professional careers and classes for students with gifts and talents) (Kunjufu, 1989). Moreover, they are often overrepresented in the less valued areas such as unemployment, school dropout rates, and special education classes (Artiles & Trent, 1994). As Ball and Harry (1993) pointed out, "One of the most obvious ways in which the special education system reflects basic inequities of the larger society is the disproportionate representation of certain populations in the students it serves—that is, in those categorized as unfit" (p. 433). Educators should not compound this problem by using materials that are not reflective of the cultural and linguistic backgrounds of learners.

Much of the impetus for multicultural education originated in the need to include accurate information about African Americans (Banks, 1993). Hilliard, Payton-Stewart, and Williams (1990) listed six generic goals for integrating multicultural content into a traditional Eurocentric curriculum identified by The First National Conference of the Infusion of African and African-American Content in the School Curriculum:

1. Students are able to understand the history of their own culture so that they know who they are and how their ancestors got into this country.
2. Teachers are able to decide how to best use curriculum materials regarding the histories of different cultural groups.
3. Students are able to acquire an interdisciplinary understanding of different cultural groups through the curriculum materials developed for all disciplines.
4. Curriculum materials such as books, videotapes, and films are acquired by schools to support curriculum infusion.
5. Community members are encouraged to participate in the infusion of curriculum and work closely with students to create curriculum resources.
6. Changes in the structure of the school and staff training are imperative to promote lasting curricular change.

Both general and special education teachers who are concerned about cultural diversity or working with students of different ethnic and cultural backgrounds should make sure that the school curriculum is consistent with these objectives. Teachers *can* influence decisions regarding the design and implementation of a school's curriculum. It is the responsibility and duty of teachers to be selective and sensitive in choosing instructional materials for their students (Duncan, 1986; Grossman, 1991). Research has indicated that teachers who participate in curriculum planning are more effective in implementing the curriculum (Baker et al., 1977), and students who receive instruction within a multicultural curriculum are more likely to develop a positive attitude about learning, themselves, and their cultures (Scarcella, 1990). The development of a positive attitude about themselves is vital for students with SED, who so often suffer with negative self-images. While multicultural education is important for *all* learners it may have additional significance for students with SED due to the disproportionate number of culturally diverse students, particularly African Americans, found in SED classroom. A multicultural curriculum can provide learners with positive examples or role models from each cultural background. The multicultural curriculum may also improve the match between the students' repertoire of behaviors and the behaviors needed for success in school.

The initial step for teachers in developing an effective multicultural curriculum is to evaluate their school's existing curriculum and determine whether the school has achieved the goals of a multicultural curriculum. For example, teachers can look at how culturally and linguistically diverse individuals are portrayed in the school's curriculum materials and observe whether students behave or talk differently as a result of being exposed to a multicultural curriculum approach. For further information on this important issue and detailed guidelines for evaluating school curricula, see Wyman (1993) and Baker and colleagues (1977).

THE IMPORTANCE OF ACADEMIC INSTRUCTION

Another critical variable in the education of students with SED is academic instruction that has a high standard of excellence. As previously indicated, SED classrooms may place limited emphasis on academic instruction (Knitzer et al., 1990). Similarly, the quality of academic instruction is often lacking in many classrooms containing students of color (Kozol, 1991). This places students of color with SED at even greater risk of being placed in a classroom in which little attention is given to academic instruction. Lack of effective academic instruction is potentially destructive for all students, but possibly even more so for students with SED, who may already be struggling with self-esteem issues. The less effective the instruc-

tion, the more the academic gap widens between students with SED and their typically developing peers. Moreover, poor instruction may further diminish students' self-confidence and increase the need for stronger social behavior controls due to student boredom and disruptive behavior. Consequently, students lack the opportunities to develop appropriate decision-making skills and self-management skills, further increasing the need for external controls. This cycle plays itself out with educators often relying on longer and harsher punishments as the students with SED progress through school until many of them—trapped in a cycle of failure—drop out. Many students with SED who drop out of school live on the fringes of society, with 73% of them being arrested within 5 years of leaving school (Osher et al., 1994).

The judicious use of behavior management techniques is important in any classroom and should include appropriate social skill instruction and appropriate consequences for inappropriate behaviors. However, effective behavior management is not the ultimate goal; it is a means to reaching the goal of developing a productive learning environment that can yield accomplished learners who are contributors to society. Behavior management and academic instruction are not mutually exclusive; they are complementary. Just as an effective classroom behavior management system can help provide an atmosphere conducive to student learning, an environment in which students are actively engaged in academics can be a tool to enhance the positive effects of a good behavior management system. For example, if a student is actively engaged in reading, writing, completing a worksheet, or responding to a teacher question, then he or she is more likely to engage in all the collateral behaviors that support that academic behavior (e.g., working quietly, thinking, and listening) (Cartledge & Milburn, 1995). The fact that students are engaged in appropriate behaviors provides their educators with additional opportunities to reinforce appropriate behaviors rather than correcting inappropriate behaviors. Bullara (1994) found that there was a decrease in off-task and disruptive behaviors of students with SED when guided notes were used during instruction. Therefore, teachers also benefit from active student participation during lessons by having a more positive teaching environment.

Researchers have found that there is a positive correlation between the amount of time students spend on academic activities and their academic achievements (Fisher, Berliner, Filby, Marliave, Cahen, & Dishaw, 1980; Greenwood et al., 1984; Heward, 1994; Roshenshine & Berliner, 1978). In other words, the higher the level of instructional engagement, the more learning and on-task behaviors will occur (Ayllon & Roberts, 1974; Broughton & Laltey, 1978; McKenzie & Henry, 1979). Subsequently, students with SED can improve their chances for success in general education classrooms.

Student-Centered Pedagogy

A dynamic educational program focuses not only on creating a culturally sensitive curriculum, but also on the identification and use of effective instructional delivery strategies. All children come to school with some experiences and skills. Unfortunately, children from diverse cultures often find that a mismatch exists between the skills they possess and the skills they need for school success. For students who also have SED, the gap between the two sets of skills becomes even wider, due to behavior problems that interfere with the learning process (Heward, 1996). It has been noted that 44% of students with SED failed one or more courses in their most recent school year, and almost half of all students with SED drop out of school (Chesapeake Institute, 1994; Valdes, Williamson, & Wagner, 1990). One technique for narrowing this gap is the student-centered pedagogy, which involves using (a) students' prior knowledge to enhance instructional materials and (b) instructional strategies that promote active student responding.

Student-centered instruction is a hallmark of special education as mandated by the Individuals with Disabilities Education Act (Public Law 101-476) and implemented through the individualized education program. Similarly, leading scholars in multicultural education have called for a student-centered focus in teaching children (Hilliard, 1989; Ladson-Billings, 1995; McGee-Banks &

Banks, 1995). Yet, there is often little guidance given to the classroom teacher beyond advocating the use of materials that reflect the diverse cultures of students in the classroom. Student-centered pedagogy also supports the use of multicultural instructional materials. However, the use of multicultural materials with the same ineffective instructional tactics may not improve the achievement of diverse learners with special needs.

One strategy that has proved effective in using students' prior knowledge as a basis for teaching new skills is the Language Experience Approach (Lee & Allen, 1963). A teacher listens and writes as a student dictates a story. The student is then asked to read the story. Because the story is from the student's own experience and in his or her own words, the student is more likely to read the words. Both the story itself and the words in the story are critical in developing literacy skills. By first learning words that are already a part of his or her verbal repertoire, the student is more apt to be successful. Using what students think and talk about can be a powerful tool in teaching academic skills. Embedding skill instruction in surroundings that are familiar to the student may enhance the learner's motivation to learn. For example, making math word problems culturally relevant could have a positive impact on students' ability to acquire new math skills. The following word problem reflects an African-American perspective:

> Rahsaan's mother sends him to the store with $10 to buy some things for dinner. She tells him if he has any money left he can buy a candy bar. The candy bar costs $.50. Rahsaan must buy 2 pounds of turnip greens and 1 pound of kale greens, both at $1 a pound. Also he needs 6 ears of corn at 6 for $1.25 and two boxes of cornbread mix at 2 for $.99. Finally, he needs a family pack of chicken. He finds one for $4.19. Does he have enough money left for a candy bar?

This example demonstrates how teachers can employ information that students already have to teach math skills. One of the misperceptions about multicultural materials is that teachers focus only on the content of the materials, rather than teaching traditional academic skills such as reading, writing, and math. In fact, academic skill instruction does take place, but with culturally sensitive instructional materials that promote high interest, motivation, and relevance to students' sociocultural, linguistic, and experiential backgrounds (Garcia & Malkin, 1993). When teachers use information that students are already familiar with in the noncritical aspects of the instructional materials, the students can focus their attention on the critical variables of the instructional materials. Using instructional materials that minimize or eliminate the elements of cultural bias should in turn provide educators with a more accurate assessment of the learners' skills.

Not only can teachers use cultural information that the learners are familiar with to enhance the instructional materials, but they can also provide further information about aspects of the students' cultures that may be unfamiliar to the students themselves. For example, they can teach weather by comparing temperature, precipitation, and seasons between where the students currently live and their ethnic countries of origin (even if the students have never lived in those countries). A teacher might have a bulletin board in the classroom with the title "Weather Around the World" and could then list countries such as Ireland, Mexico, West Africa, and China, until each student's ethnic country of origin is identified. The bulletin could list the capital city, temperature on a given day, season, and precipitation. Telling time and the addition or subtraction of time could be taught using a similar comparative strategy. Weight and distance could be instructed by comparing the pounds/feet system used in the United States compared with the metric system of various ethnic countries of origin. In addition to improving the academic performance of learners, this strategy allows the teacher to assist students with SED in developing positive self-knowledge, self-esteem, and self-ideal (Obiakor, 1994; Obiakor & Algozzine, 1995; Obiakor, Mehring, & Schwenn, 1997).

The academic skills being taught do not change, yet the child receives instruction framed in a more culturally sensitive background. This use of culturally relevant background information clearly says to the learner that his or her culture is important. While the use of culturally relevant and sensitive material is critical in the process of enriching the curriculum, its effects would be minimized without effective instruction.

Data-Based Instructional Strategies

Cooperative learning, class-wide peer tutoring, and the "low-tech" instructional strategies of choral responding, response cards, and guided notes are all examples of data-based instructional strategies that can provide increased opportunities for students to respond to curriculum materials. These student-centered strategies have been found to be effective with students both with and without disabilities (Greenwood, Hart, Walker, & Risley, 1994; Heward, 1994; Maheady, Mallette, Harper, & Sacca, 1991). Each of the strategies promotes high levels of active student responding, high rates of accurate responding, and immediate feedback.

Cooperative Learning. Cooperative learning is a teaching strategy in which students work in small groups and receive rewards or recognition based on their group performance (Slavin, 1987). Often a heterogeneous group of students work together and help one another achieve common goals and objectives. Cooperative learning has been used to teach a variety of academic and social skills to students (Goor, Schwenn, Eldridge, Mallein, & Stauffer, 1996). Research findings have indicated that cooperative learning enhances student achievement; promotes positive race relationships, as well as relationships between students with and without disabilities; increases mutual concern among students; and raises students' self-esteem (Byrd, 1995; Johnson & Johnson, 1986; Johnson, Maruyama, Johnson, Nelson, & Skon, 1981; Obiakor, 1994; Slavin, 1987). Participating students, in general, favor cooperative learning, and it does not consume too much of teachers' time (no more than 3 hours) to learn the procedures.

The results of a meta-analysis (Johnson et al., 1981) in regard to the effects of cooperative, competitive, and individualistic goal structures on achievement indicated that cooperation is superior to both competition and individualistic efforts in promoting achievement and productivity. Cooperation without intergroup competition also promotes higher achievement and productivity. This particular strategy offers a variety of advantages to teachers of students with SED. In addition to increasing active student responding to enhance academic performance, this instructional tactic provides an opportunity for students to develop problem-solving skills and improve their self-esteem, as well as interpersonal skills.

Classwide Peer Tutoring. A classwide peer tutoring research program was first developed at the Juniper Gardens Children's Project in Kansas. It was developed to improve instruction for students from disadvantaged culturally diverse backgrounds and students with learning disabilities. Increasing students' opportunities to respond, providing frequent and immediate feedback, and providing an easy delivery intervention are major characteristics of the classwide peer tutoring program. Classwide peer tutoring has been implemented successfully in a variety of settings such as mainstreamed classrooms, resource rooms, general education classrooms, and self-contained special education classrooms (Delquadri, Greenwood, Whorton, Carta, & Hall, 1986; Greenwood, Carta, & Maheady, 1991). Its procedures have been shown to be effective across different curricular areas, including mathematics, reading, spelling, word recognition, sign languages, and social studies, as well as across grade levels. Both tutors and tutees evidence academic gains and experience more positive social interactions (Osguthorpe & Scruggs, 1986). Students with disabilities, once instructed and supervised, can be effective tutors in a variety of academic content areas. In general, a classwide peer tutoring system is managed by the classroom teacher and his or her students. In most subject areas, the procedure requires about 30 minutes in which each student receives 10 minutes of tutoring (i.e., 10 minutes for each student to serve as a tutor and another 10 minutes to be the tutee). Students are assigned to a team every Monday, and they remain on this team for the entire week. Peer tutoring increases students' opportunities to respond to curriculum materials and activities. Like cooperative learning, this instructional strategy offers opportunities for students with SED to gain both academic and social skills. Reciprocal peer tutoring allows students with SED to practice giving and receiving both appropriate corrective feedback and social praise. These social skills are frequently lacking in the behavior repertoire of students with SED. Additionally, the opportunity for each student to be both a tutor and a tutee may enhance the students' self-knowledge, self-esteem, and self-ideal.

Three "Low-Tech" Teaching Strategies. Heward (1994) advocated three "low-tech" teaching strategies—choral responding, response cards, and guided notes—for increasing active student responding. According to Heward (1994), active student responding generates more learning, provides important feedback to students, and increases students' on-task behaviors. These strategies are described as a relatively "low-tech" approach because they are low cost, easy to make, durable, and hands on, and they require no special instruction prior to implementation. Choral responding requires all students in the class to respond orally in unison to teacher-posted questions. Response cards are cards, signs, or items that are held up simultaneously by all students to display their responses to a question or problem presented by the teacher. Guided notes are teacher-prepared handouts that "guide" a student through a lecture with standard cues and prepared space in which to write the key facts, concepts, and/or relationships (see Heward, 1994, for further suggestions for using these strategies).

Each low-tech strategy is empirically based, demonstrating its effectiveness in providing measurably superior gains in academic achievement across different curriculum areas such as reading, health facts, social studies, history, science, math, employment application, and driver education. Each strategy has been employed successfully in special education classrooms for students with behavior disorders, developmental disabilities, learning disabilities, and gifts and talents, and in general education classrooms and prison settings, as well as across different grade levels. Because each of these strategies promotes active student responding during lessons, the student's attention is more likely maintained for longer periods of time.

Guided notes help students follow the teacher's lecture and prompt them to write down all the important information. Many times, students with SED take inaccurate notes if they take notes at all (Bullara, 1994; Hamilton, 1991). Employing a technique that both encourages students to focus during instruction and promotes the accurate recording of information can only benefit students with SED. Similarly, response cards and choral responding tend to help sustain student participation. Both of these techniques prompt all students to respond to each teacher query during a lesson, rather than encouraging one or two more confident and/or skilled students to dominate the lesson. Once again, this is beneficial to students with SED because these strategies promote high rates of accurate responding (Gardner et al., 1994; Lockard, 1993), providing a much-needed opportunity to feel successful in school.

SUMMARY

An increasing number of students from culturally and linguistically diverse backgrounds are coming into the educational system (Grossman, 1995). These students are at a higher than usual risk for placement in special education, especially in the category of SED (CEC, 1994). Educators must continue to monitor the assessment process to prevent unnecessary placements of students from diverse cultural backgrounds into special education. Educators should increase their efforts to provide a high-quality education for all students, especially those with SED. The use of culturally sensitive materials in a curriculum that is reflective of the diversity found in schools is a critical starting point. Employment of multicultural materials can make the learning environment more student friendly.

Researchers have found that using the student's prior knowledge is an effective way to teach new skills (Heller, 1988; VanAllen, 1976). Students with SED may be more motivated when instructional materials reflect their culture in a positive manner. Moreover, the use of culturally sensitive materials may increase students' ability to understand and appropriately respond to academic materials. Culturally sensitive instructional materials may allow a better assessment of students' abilities.

Consequently, teachers can better determine and target academic skills for instruction.

However, the use of multicultural materials without the employment of effective instructional strategies may not have a significant impact on the achievement of students with SED from diverse cultures. One way to remediate this problem is to use a student-centered pedagogy. Strategies are student-centered when they use the student's prior knowledge and provide a high level of active student responding, high rate of accurate response, and immediate corrective feedback. Using the student's prior knowledge as the background for teaching new skills may increase the possibility of both mastering the materials and promoting skill retention. Empirical data indicate that there is a positive correlation between active student responding in instructional activities and student achievement level. Several student-centered strategies—cooperative learning, peer tutoring, and three "low-tech" strategies—have been found to be effective in teaching students with and without disabilities. These strategies promote positive social skills, improved academic performance, and healthy learning environments for all.

REFERENCES

Anderson, M. G., & Webb-Johnson, G. (1995). Cultural contexts, the seriously emotionally disturbed classification, and African American learners. In B. A. Ford, F. E. Obiakor, & J. M. Patton (Eds.), *Effective education of African American exceptional learners: New perspectives* (pp. 151–187). Austin, TX: Pro-Ed.

Artiles, A. J., & Trent, S. C. (1994). Overrepresentation of minority students in special education: A continuing debate. *The Journal of Special Education, 27,* 410–437.

Ayllon, T., & Roberts, M. D. (1974). Eliminating discipline problems by strengthening academic performance. *Journal of Applied Behavior Analysis, 7,* 71–76.

Baker, G. C., Browdy, M., Beecher, C., & Ho, R. P. (1977). Modifying curriculums to meet multicultural needs. In D. E. Cross, G. C. Baker, & L. J. Stiles (Eds.), *Teaching in a multicultural society: Perspectives and professional strategies* (pp. 137–153). New York: Free Press.

Ball, E., & Harry, B. (1993). Multicultural education and special education: Parallels, divergences, and intersections. *Educational Forum, 57,* 430–437.

Banks, J. A. (1993, September). Multicultural education: Progress and prospects. *Phi Delta Kappan, 75,* 21.

Barry, A. (1990). Teaching reading in a multicultural framework. *Reading Horizons, 31,* 39–47.

Bieger, E. M. (1996). Promoting multicultural education through a literature-based approach. *The Reading Teacher, 49,* 308–312.

Broughton, S. F., & Laltey, B. B. (1978). Direct and collateral effects of positive reinforcement, response cost, and mixed contingencies for academic performance. *Journal of School Psychology, 16,* 126–136.

Bullara, D. T. (1994). The effects of guided notes on the academic performance and social behaviors of students with severe behavior handicaps. Unpublished doctoral dissertation, The Ohio State University, Columbus.

Byrd, H. B. (1995). Curricular and pedagogical procedures for African American learners with academic and cognitive disabilities. In B. A. Ford, F. E. Obiakor, & J. M. Patton (Eds.), *Effective education of African American exceptional learners: New perspectives* (pp. 123–150). Austin, TX: Pro-Ed.

Cartledge, G., & Milburn, J. F. (1995). *Teaching social skills to children: Innovative approaches* (3rd ed.). New York: Pergamon.

Chesapeake Institute. (1994, September). *National agenda for achieving better results for children with serious emotional disturbance.* Washington, DC: U.S. Department of Education.

Cheng, L. L., Ima, K., & Labovitz, G. (1994). Assessment of Asian and Pacific Islander students for gifted programs. In S. B. Garcia (Ed.), *Addressing cultural and linguistic diversity in special education: Issues and trends* (pp. 30–45). Reston, VA: The Council for Exceptional Children.

Clarke, S., Dunlap, G., Foster-Johnson, L., Childs, K. E., Wilson, D., White, R., & Vera, A. (1995). Improving the conduct of students with behavioral disorders by incorporating student interests into curricular activities. *Behavioral Disorders, 20,* 221–237.

Council for Children with Behavior Disorders. (1989). Best assessment practices for students with behavioral disorders: Accommodation to cultural diversity and individual differences. *Behavioral Disorders, 14,* 263–278.

Council for Exceptional Children. (1994). Statistical profile of special education in the United States. *TEACHING Exceptional Children, 26* (Suppl. 3), 1–4.

Dean, A. V., Salend, S. J., & Taylor, L. (1993). Multicultural education: A challenge for special educators. *TEACHING Exceptional Children, 26,* 40–43.

Delquadri, J. C., Greenwood, C. R., Whorton, D., Carta, J. J., & Hall, V. R. (1986). Classwide peer tutoring. *Exceptional Children, 52,* 535–561.

Duncan, C. G. (1986). Towards a multicultural curriculum—secondary. In R. Arora & C. Duncan (Eds.), *Multicultural education: Towards good practice* (pp. 62–73). London, England: Routledge & Kegan Paul.

Fisher, C. W., Berliner, D. C., Filby, N. N., Marliave, R., Cahen, L. S., & Dishaw, M. M. (1980). Teaching behaviors, academic learning time, and student achievement: An overview. In C. Denham & A. Liebermann (Eds.), *Time to learn* (pp. 7–22), Washington, DC: National Institute of Education.

Franklin, M. E. (1992). Culturally sensitive instructional practices for African-American learners with disabilities. *Exceptional Children, 59,* 115–122.

Garcia, S. B., & Malkin, D. H. (1993). Toward defining programs and services for culturally and linguistically diverse learners in special education. *TEACHING Exceptional Children 26,* 52–58.

Gardner, R. (1990). Life space interviewing: It can be effective, but don't . . . . *Behavioral Disorders, 15,* 111–119.

Gardner, R., Heward, W. L., & Grossi, T. A. (1994). Effects of response cards on student participation and academic achievement: A systematic replication with inner-city students during whole class science instruction. *Journal of Applied Behavior Analysis, 27,* 63–71.

Goor, M., Schwenn, J., Eldridge, A., Mallein, D., & Stauffer, J. (1996, September). Using strategy cards to enhance cooperative learning for students with learning disabilities. *TEACHING Exceptional Children, 29,* 66–68.

Greenwood, C. R, Carta, J. J., & Maheady, L. (1991). Peer tutoring programs in the regular education classroom. In G. Stoner, M. R Shinn, & H. M. Walker (Eds.), *Intervention for achievement and behavior problem* (pp. 179–200). Silver Spring, MD: National Association of School Psychologists.

Greenwood, C. R., Delquadri, J., & Hall, R. V. (1984). Opportunity to respond and student academic achievement. In W. L. Heward, T. E. Heron, D. S. Hill, & J. Trap-Porter (Eds.), *Focus on behavior analysis in education* (pp. 58–88). Columbus, OH: Merrill.

Greenwood, C. R., Hart, B., Walker, D., & Risley, T. (1994). The opportunity to respond and academic performance: A behavioral theory of developmental retardation and its prevention. In R. Gardner et al. (Eds.), *Behavior analysis in education: Focus on measurably superior instruction* (pp. 213–223). Pacific Grove, CA: Brooks/Cole.

Grossman, H. (1991). Special education in a diverse society: Improving services for minority and working class students. *Preventing School Failure, 36,* 19–27.

Grossman, H. (1995). *Teaching in a diverse society.* Boston: Allyn & Bacon.

Hamilton, S. L. (1991). *Effects of guided notes on academic performance of incarcerated juvenile delinquents with learning disabilities.* Unpublished masters thesis, The Ohio State University, Columbus.

Heller, M. F. (1988). Comprehending and composing through language experience. *The Reading Teacher, 42,* 130–135.

Heward, W. L. (1994). Three "low-tech" strategies for increasing the frequency of active student response during group instruction. In R. Gardner et al. (Eds.), *Behavior analysis in education: Focus on measurably superior instruction* (pp. 283–320). Pacific Grove, CA: Brooks/Cole.

Heward, W. L. (1996). *Exceptional children: An introduction to special education* (5th ed.). Englewood Cliffs, NJ: Prentice Hall.

Hilliard, A. G. (1989). Back to Binet: The case against the use of IQ tests in the schools. *Diagnostique, 14,* 125–135.

Hilliard, L. L. (1995). Defining the "multi-" in "multicultural" through children's literature. *The Reading Teacher, 48,* 728–730.

Hilliard, A. G., Payton-Stewart, L., & Williams, L. O. (Eds.). (1990). *Infusion of African and African American content in the school curriculum.* Morristown, NJ: Aaron Press.

Johnson, D. W., & Johnson, R. T. (1986). Mainstreaming and cooperative learning strategies. *Exceptional Children, 52,* 553–561.

Johnson, D. W., Maruyama, G., Johnson, R., Nelson, D., & Skon, L. (1981). The effects of cooperative, competitive, and individualistic goal structures on achievement: A meta-analysis. *Psychological Bulletin, 89,* 47–62.

Knitzer, J., Steinberg, Z., & Flesch, B. (1990). *At the schoolhouse door: An examination of programs and policies for children with behavioral and emotional problems.* New York: Bank Street.

Kozol, J. (1991). *Savage inequalities: Children in America's schools.* New York: Crown.

Kunjufu, J. (1989). *Critical issues in educating African American youth: A talk with Jawanza.* Chicago: African American Images.

Ladson-Billings, G. (1995). But that's just good teaching! The case for culturally relevant pedagogy. *Theory into Practice, 34,* 159–165.

Lee, D. M., & Allen, R. V. (1963). *Learning to read through experience* (2nd ed.). New York: Appleton-Century-Crofts.

Lockard, L. (1993, August). *Effects of choral responding and response cards on academic achievement by students during large group social studies instruction.* Unpublished master's thesis, The Ohio State University, Columbus.

Maheady, L., Mallette, B., Harper, G., & Sacca, F. (1991). Heads together: A peer mediated option for improving the academic achievement of heterogeneous learning groups. *Remedial and Special Education, 12,* 45–56.

McGee-Banks, C. A., & Banks, J. (1995). Equity pedagogy: An essential component of multicultural education. *Theory into Practice, 34,* 152–158.

McKenzie, G. R., & Henry, M. (1979). Effects of testlike events on on-task behavior, test anxiety, and achievement in a classroom rule-learning task. *Journal of Educational Psychology, 71,* 370–374.

Midgette, T. E. (1995). Assessment of African American exceptional learners: New strategies and perspectives. In B. A. Ford, F. E. Obiakor, & J. M. Patton (Eds.), *Effective education of African American exceptional learners: New perspectives* (pp. 3–25). Austin, TX: Pro-Ed.

National Mental Health Association. (1993). *All systems fail.* Washington DC: Author.

Obiakor, F. E. (1994). *The eight step multicultural approach: Learning and teaching with a smile.* Dubuque, IA: Kendall/Hunt.

Obiakor, F. E., & Algozzine, B. (1995). *Managing problem behaviors: Perspectives for general and special educators.* Dubuque, IA: Kendall/Hunt.

Obiakor, F. E., Mehring, T. A., & Schwenn, J. O. (1997). *Disruptions, disasters, and death: Helping students deal with crisis.* Reston, VA: The Council for Exceptional Children.

Osher, D., Osher, T. , & Smith, C. (1994). Toward a national perspective in emotional and behavioral disorders: A developmental agenda. *Beyond Behavior, 6,* 6–17.

Osguthorpe, R. T., & Scruggs, T. E. (1986). Special education students as tutors: A review and analysis. *Remedial and Special Education, 7,* 15–25.

Pallas, A. M., Natriella, G., & McDill, E. L. (1989). The changing nature of the disadvantaged population: Current dimensions and future trends. *Educational Researcher, 18,* 16–22.

Roshenshine, B., & Berliner, D. C. (1978). Academic engaged time. *British Journal of Teacher Education, 4,* 3–16.

Scarcella, R. (1990). *Teaching language minority students in the multicultural classroom.* Englewood Cliffs, NJ: Prentice-Hall

Sizemore, B. A. (1990). The politics of curriculum, race, and class. *Journal of Negro Education, 59,* 77–84.

Slavin, R. E. (1987). Synthesis of research on cooperative learning. *Educational Leadership, 48,* 72–82.

Sugai, G., & Maheady, L. (1988). Cultural diversity and individual assessment for behavior disorders. *TEACHING Exceptional Children, 21,* 28–31.

United States Department of Education. (1994, September). National agenda for achieving better results for children and youth with serious emotional disturbances. Washington, DC: Office of Special Education Programs.

Valdes, K. A., Williamson, C. L., & Wagner, M. (1990). Youth categorized as emotionally disturbed. In K. A. Valdes, C. L. Williamson, & M. Wagner (Eds.), *A statistical almanac: The national longitudinal transition study of special education students, Vol. 3.* Menlo Park, CA: SRI International.

VanAllen, R. U. (1976). *Language experience in communication.* Boston: Houghton Mifflin.

Walker, H. M., & Bullis, M. (1991). Behavior disorders and social context of regular class integration: A conceptual dilemma. In J. W. Lloyd, W. Singh, & A. C. Repp (Eds.), *The regular education initiatives: Alternative perspectives on issues and models* (pp. 75–93). Sycamore, IL: Sycamore.

Williams, L. R. (1989). Multicultural programs, curricula, and strategies. In P. G. Ramsey, E. B. Vold, & L. R. Williams (Eds.), *Multicultural education: A source book* (pp. 79–117). New York: Garland.

Wyman, S. L. (1993). *How to respond to your culturally diverse student population.* Alexandria, VA: Association for Supervision and Curriculum Development.

ABOUT THE AUTHORS

BRIAN KAI YUNG TAM, Assistant Professor, Kean College, New Jersey. RALPH GARDNER, III, Associate Professor, The Ohio State University.

Preparation of this article was supported by a Leadership Training Grant (H029D10054) from the U.S. Department of Education, Office of Special Education and Rehabilitation Services. Correspondence concerning this article should be addressed to Ralph Gardner, III or Brian Kai Yung Tam, Department of Educational Services and Research, College of Education, The Ohio State University, Room 356, Arps Hall, 1945 High Street, Columbus, Ohio 43210. Electronic mail may be sent via internet to ragardne@magnus.acs.ohio-state.edu or ktam@magnus.acs.ohio-state.edu.

Ethnic Minority Scholars Writing for Professional Publication: From Myth to Reality

FRED SPOONER
BOB ALGOZZINE
University of North Carolina Charlotte

MARTHA THURLOW
University of Minnesota

FESTUS OBIAKOR
Emporia State University

BILL HELLER
University of South Florida

ABSTRACT: *Writing for publication is a professional development necessity for most college and university faculty members. Many argue that scholars from ethnic minority groups do not publish at the level they probably should. In this article, we discuss reasons for this and provide some remedies for it. First, we explore myths and misconceptions about professional writing that detract from productivity and counter them with some realities that we have discovered about successful writing. We then offer some suggestions as to how to make writing part of a regularly scheduled activity to increase the likelihood that productive writing will be done. We close with perspectives from ethnic minority scholars themselves on writing in support of cultural and linguistic diversity and special education.*

Life for special education faculty members from ethnic minority groups typically revolves around a tenure and promotion system that includes three components: research, teaching, and service. The degree to which any one of these components is weighted more heavily than the others sometimes depends on the type of university where the faculty member is employed (e.g., Research University I, Research University II, Doctoral I, Doctoral II, Master's Comprehensive I) (cf. The Carnegie Foundation for the Advancement of Teaching, 1994). Sometimes a well-articulated statement directs interaction and integration among these areas of opportunity for professional development More often, few guidelines are provided and faculty play a never-ending guessing game (O'Toole, 1994):

> [O]ne of the most unsettling characteristics of the dominant tenure practices is a system of moving standards. When the young professor asks how many scholarly articles one must list on a vita to qualify for tenure, the common reply is "*n* + 2." In other words:

"However many you have, it will take two more." (p. 82)

Despite continuing questions and ongoing debate about the specifics of the tenure and promotion process, the benefits of these professional development activities are seldom questioned. Reputational information is an important outcome that is used by potential and current employees and students to make decisions about seeking employment or attending a particular university based on its programmatic offerings (Eash, 1983; Sindelar & Schloss, 1986). As universities attempt to upgrade their status within a state university structure (e.g., moving from a Master's Comprehensive classification to a Doctoral or Research classification) or improve their status in the national rankings of institutions within their level of classification, faculty publications claim an important position as evidence that contributes to these evaluations. Consequently, as young faculty members move into the system, conversations about professional development, especially in areas related to scholarship and writing, are inevitable. Clearly, disseminating information (e.g., professional presentations, published articles in refereed journals) is another important agenda item for scholars from ethnic minority groups who seek and want to maintain employment in higher education.

REALITIES, OTHER RESPONSIBILITIES, AND OBSTACLES

Conducting research and disseminating research findings *are* important activities for university faculty, but they have other responsibilities as well: (a) teaching classes; (b) advising students; (c) holding scheduled office hours; (d) conducting service activities (e.g., working with principals, teachers, schools, and children in a direct hands-on capacity); and (e) discharging other university-related responsibilities (e.g., attending to committee assignments, department faculty meetings, and curriculum revision). With the assignment of these other important academic responsibilities, how is it possible to find time to write, especially when faced daily with the constant bombard-

ment from life's other little skirmishes, conflicts, and battles? We all know the scenario too well:

You start out the day with good intentions and some semblance of a schedule with class at 3:00 P.M.; a lecture to prepare for that day, perhaps even to be delivered at 3:00 P.M.; a departmental meeting starting at 12:30 P.M. and lasting until 2:00 P.M.; a few scheduled student appointments; an ongoing weekly curriculum revision committee meeting starting at 10:00 A.M. and perhaps lasting until 11:30 A.M. (this committee will likely meet for the duration of the semester and perhaps this committee or a similar one with a parallel format for the entire academic year); and yes, there are these data you have collected that you really want to attempt to disseminate. You plan to work on conceptualizing your manuscript at 8:00 A.M. That would give you 2 hours before any externally imposed scheduled activity. You get to the office at 8:30 A.M. (traffic on your regular route to work was extremely slow this morning). When you arrive—late of course—there is a throng of students waiting at your office door (you have the midterm scheduled for next week). You have not even been able to open the morning mail or check your E-mail, but you really need to spend time with the students anxiously waiting outside your door. It should be no surprise that your scheduled writing time for that day just disappeared. Maybe tomorrow will be the day you write the article—but don't count on it!

Although responsibilities such as teaching classes and advising students are important, sometimes tasks related to them are more easily undertaken and completed than those associated with writing. In many cases, the immediacy associated with other assignments distracts even the most well-intentioned and organized professor from sitting down and writing. Couple this reality with evidence indicating that faculty with diverse cultural and ethnic backgrounds face additional "cultural taxation" (e.g., being called upon to be the expert in matters of diversity, possibly without experience or knowledge about the role; serving on affirmative action committees or cultural awareness task forces; and representing the department in all matters related to diversity), and a troubling observation emerges (Padilla, 1994, p.26). Being successful and productive in professional writing is a hallmark of success within the university community, and too often the evidence of productivity among ethnic minority faculty is less than abundant.

Enhancing the presence and contributions of members from diverse cultural and linguistic groups has been a professional concern in the education community for some time. The changing demographics of schools in the United States, as well as the emphasis on reform and restructuring efforts to address the needs of all students, has kept the concern alive in recent years. African Americans, American Indians, Asian Americans, and Hispanic Americans comprise about a third of the school-age population and are a majority in many urban school districts (Ysseldyke & Algozzine, 1995). Although programs have been developed to address these concerns and needs, they have fallen short in their overall effects. And, "even with the best efforts . . . to enhance the role of minorities . . . in . . . the research community, there remains the extraordinarily critical 'pipeline problem'" (Russell, 1994, p. 27).

One of the key reasons ethnic minority scholars are underrepresented is that professional systems fall to retain them at all points in the education continuum. The number of members of diverse cultural and linguistic groups entering research and postsecondary teaching careers is tragically small. Many special education faculty from these groups who are entering research and postsecondary teaching careers are not prepared to meet expectations in areas related to faculty development and professional writing (Russell, 1994). Padilla (1994) commented that even if people of color and research professionals from diverse ethnic groups are prepared to meet faculty development expectations, they frequently encounter a dilemma as to the degree to which their ethnic research will be valued by colleagues, can be published in refereed journals, and will be judged to be of significant enough scientific merit to earn tenure and promotion.

We have found that barriers that impede the success of ethnic minority faculty in professional writing can be overcome. This article examines myths and misconceptions about writing, offers some suggestions as to how to write on a more consistent basis, and shares observations from ethnic minority scholars on productive approaches to professional writing.

DEBUNKING MYTHS AND MISCONCEPTIONS

Henson (1995) identified six myths that harm potential writers. They are as follows:

1. I'm not sure I have what it takes.
2. I don't have time to write.
3. I don't have anything worth writing about.
4. The editors will reject my manuscript because my name is not familiar to them.
5. My vocabulary and writing skills are too limited.
6. In my field there are few opportunities to publish.

These myths can be dangerous to writers from ethnic minority backgrounds because they have broad self-concept and productivity implications. Writing is hard work, and perceptions that detract from our willingness to do it just make it more difficult. We concur with Henson's statement that "good writers are self-made, not born" (p. 24). Faculty members from minority groups have messages. They must tell their stories. Here are some observations to help put writing on the approach, rather than avoidance, track:

1. Since we all have stories to tell, we all have what it takes to be good writers. We must be self-motivated and self-empowered to write.
2. We make time for whatever we like to do. We cannot dismiss the inconsistencies in our history unless we make time to write.
3. There are many issues confronting us. These issues are worth writing about.
4. Everyone's manuscript can be rejected. No one is immune from rejection. Rejection of a person's manuscript does not in any way mean rejection of that person.
5. We improve our vocabulary and writing skills by writing. Remember, writers are self-made, not born.
6. There are many opportunities for people from diverse cultural and linguistic backgrounds. Today, almost all professional conferences and publications focus on issues facing these groups. Since our demograph-

ics are changing, these issues cannot be swept under the rug.

7. We must enjoy the power that writing brings. To decry tokenism, we must enjoy the power associated with publication of books, monographs, articles, and other forms of writing. We cannot continue to be victims. We must define ourselves through our works.

8. We must collaborate, consult, and cooperate with people. Writing enhances teamwork and teamwork enhances writing. Individuals in different institutions can have similar interests and different perspectives that enrich written products.

9. Our freedoms are incomplete unless we express them. An important medium for such expression is writing.

In our own experience, we have come across additional myths that are potentially dangerous to developing writers. Here are some of them and a brief discussion of what really happens in writing for professional publication:

Myth: A rejected article is not good.
Reality: A rejected article needs to be revised and resubmitted.
Myth: Good research always gets published.
Reality: Persistent authors usually get published.

Too often, neophyte writers take rejection too literally. Very often, manuscripts are rejected for reasons related to issues other than quality. For example, editors often reject manuscripts because recent journal issues have contained similar material or a manuscript simply is not appropriate for their readership. Good advice: If appropriate, use reviewer comments to revise what you have written and submit it to another journal within 1 week of a rejection. Give yourself a chance to be published in at least five different journals before accepting a final rejection. All successful writers have been faced with having a manuscript rejected. Researcher Louis Pasteur indicated that part of his strength was his tenacity to continue in the face of rejection and failure. F. Scott Fitzgerald covered his bedroom walls with 122 rejection letters that he had received (Kiewra, 1994).

Myth: Heavy hitters publish 30 to 40 articles a year.

Reality: Heavy hitters probably submit 5 or 6 articles a year and most will be accepted and published.

Many people resist writing because they hold unrealistic standards for how much they should be publishing. Often this results in a limited record of writing (cf. Baker & Wilson, 1992; Roush, Williams, & Luna, 1995). Set realistic expectations for your writing: One to two articles a year when you are starting your career is an appropriate goal. If you do no other writing during your early years of college teaching, turn your dissertation into at least one manuscript submitted for publication. If you do nothing else when adjusting your writing aspirations, avoid "paralysis by analysis." Time spent deciding how much or how many to write is time not spent actually writing.

Myth: You have to be brilliant to publish articles.
Reality: You have to write to publish articles.

Most successful writers spend a lot of time writing. They recognize the benefits of practice to the improvement of their skills. They accept the courage it takes to submit their writing to external review and welcome the opportunities to make something they have written better. These are characteristics associated with people who like to write. Kiewra (1994) suggested that continued work increases and enhances creative output. Career length is only one measure of a writer's success; the daily investment of time is also important. Spend the first portion of each day (or another part that is more suitable to your schedule) writing.

Myth: There is one right way to write.
Reality: There are many ways to write, but some are better than others.

Regardless of what you believe about writing or how you address the myths that surround it, there are some fundamentals in the discipline of writing that help bring it more convincingly to life.

ENHANCING WRITING SKILLS

Most individuals in higher education who have been successful at "professoring" have found ways to schedule and budget their time and somehow or other are able to write manuscripts that get published. These successful professors either have developed their own contingency management system for getting the job done or have followed one of the many suggestions on writing that can be found in the literature (e.g., Henson, 1995; Spooner & Heller, 1993; Wallace, 1977). Although our purpose is to assist and encourage those who are still struggling and have not found a workable set of contingencies, there may also be some helpful hints here for the seasoned veteran.

B. F. Skinner, perhaps one of the most prolific writers in higher education within the fields of psychology and education, also has shared his secrets for successful writing. Skinner's (1981) recommendations for *How to Discover What You Have to Say* are simple, eloquent, practical, understandable, and easily implemented: Put yourself in the best physical condition to write; control the conditions under which writing will occur; have a mechanism to capture related information; stay out of prose as long as possible; indicate valid relationships among the parts by constructing an outline; and construct the prose draft loosely.

Condition Yourself to Write

Although there is nothing earth-shattering about conducting your daily activities in a fashion that provides for appropriate rest, exercise, and diet, many times the "midnight oil" is burned in combination with an early rise the next morning to meet some type of externally imposed deadline. Most of us involved in higher education, from students studying for final examinations to professors attempting to meet grant deadline submissions, have violated the tenets of this recommendation. As long as there are deadlines and humans attempting to meet those deadlines, there will be some modification of optimal physical conditioning. Yet, most of us do not do our best work under those stretched conditions. Rest is important to keep from periodically dozing on the job. Diet helps to keep your physical system running regularly. Exercise of some kind, at some level, on a regular basis is also recommended to reduce stress.

Control Conditions for Writing

Skinner's second recommendation, in part, speaks to the issue of scheduling and the location for writing. Although most professors have offices at the university, for some people this location may not be the optimum site for writing. An office located at home may provide a better writing environment.

As we approach the 21st century, many people use computer hardware and word-processing software for writing and other professional tasks. In addition to the computer, access to reference materials (e.g., professional journals, books, etc.) is important. Your writing environment should be arranged so that you have access to everything you need to perform the task at hand and a space that is large enough to lay out the materials you need in a logical, systematic format, so that citations can be located, stored, and retrieved without having to spend undue time digging through piles of irrelevant material to find the information you need to write the next sentence.

It is also important to establish a specific time each day when you will write. Randomly trying to find the time to write and meeting other priorities (answering the phone, meetings, etc.), will constantly supersede your good intentions. *Make the time!* Set aside 2 hours, have a place where you will write, and write consistently. During your writing sessions do not try to do too much at one time. You may need to build up your time to 2 hours instead of starting with a 2-hour time period and trying to find a way to fill the time. When the session is concluded, do something unrelated (e.g., teach class, exercise, advise students).

Capture Related Information

It is important to have a mechanism to capture related information when you are not in your controlled writing environment at the office or at home. You do not have to be at your writing desk exclusively to have an idea about something you want to say. Thoughts will likely come to you when you are involved in other activities. A question raised by a student in class may be relevant to the section of the manuscript that you were just addressing this morning. You may be attempting to go to sleep, and an idea about a project on which you are working will come forward. Making notes that probably only you can understand is a good way to record information that comes to you at odd times. Jot down the information on whatever may be handy, and file it using whatever system works for you so that you can use it later. Keeping track of your ideas and having a mechanism through which those ideas can be retrieved will expedite your writing time, make you a more effective writer, and allow you the opportunity to wrestle with difficult sections of writing tasks "off line," with a reliable way to recover the information.

Stay Out of Prose

A fourth recommendation is not to attempt to sit down and write the perfect first sentence. This suggestion might best be portrayed by an example of how not to do it. Imagine a scenario with a trash can overflowing with wadded-up paper, an individual with a sweating brow, a perplexed look on her face, and a clock on the wall, ticking . . . ticking, with a caption that says something like, "Only 2 hours until deadline!" Important parts of what you have to say can be manipulated more easily if they are parts of sentences—just words. Get your thoughts down on paper. Take one component of your paper—let's say the introduction section, or more specifically, the purpose statement. Without writing a complete sentence, you may start with a word or a sentence fragment (the spelling at this point does not even need to be correct) and put the idea on paper or the computer screen. You have made a start, an important first step. As you continually refine the thoughts you have captured in fragment and note form, the information will accumulate and you can arrange it in different orders to expound upon your idea.

Construct an Outline

Once you have a few notes on paper or the screen (e.g., your purpose statement), you may use those notes to develop an idea with subordinate points to support and elaborate the heading. For example, your purpose statement can provide a basis for developing key components of your message. You may say to yourself,

"There are three major purposes to the research study, (1) . . ., (2) . . ., and (3) . . ." "The current study is related to the specific body of previous literature in four ways." Now you can begin to see the parts of your introduction take shape before your eyes.

This outline is only for your purposes and will not be published, so use it freely. Information can be added to or deleted from the outline. Computer hardware and word-processing software may be useful in the outlining stage and also save time as you begin to develop the first draft. Components of the outline can be expanded, and moved if necessary, as the first draft takes shape. Citations that help substantiate specific material may also be part of the outlining process. With the outline in place, you can then develop an idea (when it actually comes time to write sentences and paragraphs) and devote total attention to the way in which the sentence is phrased, referring to the outline only to pick up the next point. Now that the ideas are on paper and you have indicated an order in which to present those ideas, it is time to begin to put together the first draft.

Construct Drafts Loosely

After you have an outline of sufficient detail— enough information that you can begin to elaborate on your points—begin to put the information into sentences and paragraphs. Yet it is still important not to get too concerned about the structure of the material. Skinner's sixth recommendation is to construct the prose draft loosely. Just focus on getting the information down on paper. Do not try to make your words perfect the first time around. This first attempt at actually putting the words into a prose format is just that—a first draft. You may want to write the whole document as a rough draft or write one section at a time (e.g., just the introduction). After the first sketch of the introduction is written, go back and review it thoroughly. Examine the sentence structure, the word usage, the flow between sentences, and the continuity between paragraphs. If you are co-authoring a paper with a colleague, with each of you writing different sections, write your section and then let your partner read it. At this juncture the words are on paper, and you are using your writing time to review, revise, and edit.

Although all six of Skinner's points are important, controlling the conditions under which writing will occur may be the most important. If other prominent tasks regularly take precedence over writing, you will never complete the manuscript (and even the best data are of limited value if they remain in the bottom of a file drawer). If you do not schedule time to write on a frequent basis, if you just try to work it in at odd times or at times when you are not so busy with your other tasks, you may never start the manuscript. Making time to write on a consistent daily basis, in an environment that is conducive to writing, is critical to telling the stories that will broaden and enhance the lives of learners from culturally and linguistically diverse backgrounds.

PERSPECTIVES FROM ETHNIC MINORITY SCHOLARS

Our examination of selected elementary textbooks, grades 1 to 6, disclosed that the historical background and cultural contributions of slaves in early America are ignored. In particular, the art, architecture, literature, and music contributed by West Africans during their enslavement in the American South are excluded. (Thomas & Alawiye, 1990, p. 20)

This statement underscores three major points for ethnic minority writers. First, there is a dearth of information about the positive experiences of people from diverse cultural and linguistic backgrounds in our media, textbooks, journals, magazines, newsletters, and newspapers. Second, stories with a minority perspective cannot be told accurately unless professionals with minority experiences attempt to tell them. Third, telling these stories through discourse without accurate written records does a great disservice to those whose stories are being told. It is true that sources of the history of minority groups include oral tradition, archaeological evidence, royal emblem, and written documents, but it is also true that among these sources, written documents appear to be the most reliable. When stories are passed orally from person to person their accuracy begins to dwindle, but when they are writ-

ten, they endure the test of time. As Ricoeur (1976) pointed out, "Writing is the full manifestation of discourse" (pp. 25–26). In other words, to persons from culturally and linguistically diverse backgrounds, writing must be taken seriously. It not only tells our stories, but also buttresses teaching, scholarship, and service to minority communities (Lamb, 1986).

Why Should We Write?

Scholars who are members of ethnic minority groups should take seriously the question of how we can complain about our representation in the literature if we do not tell our stories in writing. In his book *The Art of Writing for Publication*, Henson (1995) categorized individuals into two groups: talkers and doers. Talkers spend considerable time discussing what they will write or defending why they do not write. Doers have goals for writing and spend their time producing written products. Clearly the easier task is talking, but doing is probably more rewarding, and it is more difficult to ignore even a mundane permanent product than a brilliantly conceived and delivered lecture or discourse.

There are many reasons why ethnic minority scholars should write. When you are a writer, "you are very much your own boss. You can decide what you want to write, when you want to write it, and even where you want to write" (Henson, 1995, p. 3). Writers are creative individuals whose talents offer tremendous professional opportunities for growth. Writing helps individuals to clarify their own thinking. Myriad issues affecting learners from culturally and linguistically diverse backgrounds cannot be resolved simplistically. Writing about them creates and continues dialogs that can bring about change.

Professionals in special education are continuously challenged to respond to a multitude of issues related to cultural and linguistic diversity and teaching. Some of these concerns are: (a) intelligence quotients of students from ethnic minority groups, (b) the underrepresentation of these groups in programs for gifted students, (c) their overrepresentation in programs for persons with cognitive disabilities, and (d) the inclusion of minority students with exceptionalities in regular programs. Equally important are widely addressed classroom instructional issues: (a) the lack of persons from ethnic minority groups in teacher education programs, (b) the recruitment and retention of persons from minority groups in school programs, (c) the limited recognition and use of teaching techniques for students from culturally and linguistically diverse backgrounds, and (d) limited understanding of differences in learning styles and appropriate problem solving. Many of these issues have been addressed from only the mainstream Anglo-American perspective. They need to be addressed from other cultural perspectives as well. They cannot be resolved through unidimensional discourse or rhetoric alone. Henson (1995) argued, "Writing is a proactive endeavor, and nobody can be forced to write. People write because they choose to" (p. 3). We cannot resolve inconsistencies in our thinking unless we write, and we cannot resolve inconsistencies in the literature unless we write. The old adage that "talk is cheap" might be too simplistic; however, no amount of discourse or rhetoric can remediate the inconsistencies in our history, values, and stories unless we write them down to become part of our literature.

On Writing Well

People learn to write by writing. There are successful scholars and teachers from diverse cultural and ethnic groups who can become mentors; there are also Anglo-American colleagues who can brighten the way. These successful people did not become successful in one day; they became successful through hard work and dedication. They know the benefits of working with others and frequently are willing to collaborate, share, and support. In the long run, these successful individuals enrich themselves and others through their works. In addition to financial remuneration in the forms of tenure, promotion, or merit pay, they receive personal gratification for their work. As Henson (1995) has pointed out, writing is empowering.

Many university programs survive today because of the writing efforts of their faculties. Funded grant proposals and manuscripts published in professional journals provide evidence of successful writing efforts. Most proposals will not be funded unless they are well written and well targeted to address current problems. Some knowledge base and technical skills are required to produce a good grant proposal. Results of these grants are in turn published as books, book chapters, and research articles to increase visibility. Thus, it is a "win–win" situation when scholars from ethnic minority backgrounds write. Henson (1995) has suggested that a skilled writer can change the behavior of many people.

CONCLUSION

Writing is hard work. It requires persistent effort to fight against the insecurity engendered by myths and the inadequacies evident in most advanced degree preparation programs. Scholars from ethnic minority backgrounds win battles against these villains with support, encouragement, and continuing development of skills related to successful professional writing. Kiewra (1994) offered the following six guidelines for publishing without perishing:

1. Study a domain intensively.
2. Confront challenging and important goals.
3. Conduct systematic work with colleagues.
4. Write clearly and with style.
5. Embrace feedback.
6. Do not lose perspective.

His message is echoed in what we believe is central to good professional writing by members of ethnic minority groups: Confront myths with reality, develop a writing style, and choose writing topics that foster and support goals that are important to these groups. To help put it all into practice, run two tests on your next written product. First, adapt Kiewra's "kid test" (1994, p. 31): Ask yourself whether what you are writing about will advance knowledge about people with exceptionalities and broaden perspectives on cultural diversity and progress of people from ethnic minority backgrounds. If not, write something that will. Second, adapt Levin's "friend test" (1992, p. 14): Ask friends outside of work to read what you have written. If they cannot tell you what it is about, rewrite it until they can.

University faculty members with minority ethnic backgrounds do not write as much as they should, and there are numerous reasons why this is so. Two reasons were addressed in detail in this article: (1) Many scholars from ethnic minority backgrounds have been unduly influenced by myths and misconceptions about professional writing, and (2) many have not received adequate training in the discipline of writing. We have debunked a number of myths about professional writing by discussing some of its realities. It appears from our analysis that *scheduled persistence* is a key component to personally dissolving many of the misconceptions about professional writing and publishing. Skinner's (1981) recommendations for finding a way to say what you have to say are an excellent basis for developing and extending essential writing skills. We hope what we have written will encourage scholars from minority backgrounds to become regular contributors to special education's literature, to tell their stories more frequently and accurately, and to let their voices be heard in support of learners who are culturally and linguistically diverse.

REFERENCES

Baker, D. R., & Wilson, M. V. K. (1992). An evaluation of the scholarly productivity of doctoral candidates. *Journal of Social Work Education, 28,* 204–213.

The Carnegie Foundation for the Advancement of Teaching. (1994). *A technical report: A classification of institutions of higher education.* Princeton: Author.

Eash, M. (1983). Educational research productivity of institutions of higher education. *American Educational Research Journal, 20,* 5–12.

Henson, K. T. (1995). *The art of writing for publication.* Boston: Allyn and Bacon.

Kiewra, K. A. (1994). A slice of advice. *Educational Researcher, 23*(3), 31–33.

Lamb, C. E. (1986). Using research results in the university classrooms. *Proceedings of the Second Regional Conference on University Teaching* (pp. 519–523). Las Cruces, NM: New Mexico State University.

O'Toole, J. (1994, May/June). Tenure: A conscientious objection. *Change, 26,* 79–87.

Padilla, A. M. (1994). Ethnic minority scholars, research, and mentoring: Current and future issues. *Educational Researcher, 23*(4), 24–27.

Ricoeur, P. (1976). *Interpretation theory: Discourse and the surplus of meaning.* Fort Worth: The Texas Christian University Press.

Roush, R. E., Williams, M. G., & Luna, M. (1995). Scholarly productivity levels of nursing faculty in a geriatrics education program. *Nursing Education, 34,* 175–176.

Russell, W. J. (1994). Achieving diversity in academe: AERA's role. *Educational Researcher, 23*(9), 26–28.

Sindelar, P. T., & Schloss, P. J. (1986). The reputations of doctoral training programs in special education. *The Journal of Special Education, 20,* 49–59.

Skinner, B. F. (1981). How to discover what you have to say: A talk to students. *The Behavior Analyst, 4,* 1–8.

Spooner, F., & Heller, H. W. (1993). Writing for publication in journals for practitioners: Suggestions for teachers and early career researchers. *Remedial and Special Education, 14*(3), 47–52.

Thomas, J. I., & Alawiye, O. (1990, September). *American elementary school texts: Dignity for Blacks?* Paper presented at the National Social Science Association (NSSA) Conference, Washington, DC.

Wallace, I. (1977). Self-control techniques of famous novelists. *Journal of Applied Behavior Analysis, 10,* 515–525.

Ysseldyke, J. E., & Algozzine, B. (1995). *Special education: A practical approach for teachers.* Boston: Houghton Mifflin.

ABOUT THE AUTHORS

FRED SPOONER, Professor, University of North Carolina at Charlotte. BOB ALGOZZINE, Professor of Teaching Specialities, College of Education and Allied Professions, University of North Carolina at Charlotte. MARTHA THURLOW, Research Professor, Department of Educational Psychology, University of Minnesota. FESTUS OBIAKOR, Professor of Special Education, Division of Psychology/Special Education, Emporia State University. BILL HELLER, Dean, University of South Florida-St. Petersburg.

Success with a Student with Limited English Proficiency: One Teacher's Experience

WHITNEY HOSMER RAPP

Michigan State University

ABSTRACT: This article investigates one way in which teachers can help students with limited English proficiency (LEP) be successful in English-speaking classrooms. The principles of the Early Literacy Project reflect what researchers have found to be beneficial for students with LEP. The case study of a Vietnamese-speaking fourth grader placed in special education is examined here. Data, including pre- and posttest scores, student work samples, videotaped classroom observations, and audiotaped teacher and student interviews, were collected over the course of 1 year. Results of quantitative and qualitative data analysis show that while the student has not made significant gains in all areas, he has shown considerable growth in language acquisition and literacy development.

Educators are becoming more concerned with the literacy instruction of students from culturally and linguistically diverse backgrounds. The increasing population of these students exacerbates this concern. Between 1986 and 1991, the population of students with limited English proficiency (LEP) increased by 52% (Fix & Zimmerman, 1993). By 1992, there were 2.6 million students with LEP in the United States (McKeon, 1994). Although the number of students with LEP is growing, the number of programs helping them to achieve is not. These students are 1.5 times more likely to drop out of school than are their English-proficient peers (McCollum, 1991). Even though some students with LEP have been successful in some schools, there seems to be a lingering question of why so many more of them fall through the cracks and drop out of school.

One reason is that students with LEP often experience a conflict between the language, traditions, and values at home and those at school (Miramontes & Commins, 1991).

Teachers become frustrated with their own inability to meet the needs of these students and distance themselves from them. Parents, who remember the negative experiences of their own schooling and are apprehensive about approaching educators, distance themselves from their children's education. Students perceive this distance as disapproval or rejection. They feel they are disappointing their parents by wanting to do well in school and disappointing their teachers by holding on to their native language, values, and traditions (Miramontes & Commins, 1991).

This article is motivated by the need to find ways to help students from culturally and linguistically diverse backgrounds succeed in school without leaving behind the cultural traditions and values they bring from the home. There is a need to develop instructional programs that help students feel confident in school even though they are from a different background. In these programs, diversity must be viewed as a strength rather than a deficit.

THE ISSUE

Researchers have agreed that an emphasis on native language needs to be a component of instructional programs if they are to be successful with students with LEP (Chiang, 1994; Cummins, 1989; Fradd & Correa, 1989; Gersten & Woodward, 1994; Goldenberg, 1992; Leo, 1994; Miramontes & Cummins, 1991; Poplin & Phillips, 1993; Stein, 1986). Providing students with instruction in their native languages as they learn English as a second language can instill in them a feeling of pride in their heritage, as well as help them succeed academically. It takes from 5 to 7 years of second language instruction for a student to be able to function cognitively in that language (Cummins, 1989). If support in the native language lasts this long, students with LEP will not lag in content area subjects while working to acquire English as a second language (Chiang, 1994).

However, it is not possible for all students with LEP to be taught in their native languages. It is estimated that 88% of the teachers in the United States are Caucasian. Of preservice teachers, fewer than 5% speak more than one language fluently, and three fifths are completely monolingual (Cushner, McClelland, & Safford, 1992). With the increasing number of students with LEP in the United States every year, these preservice teachers will need to know how to provide them with the academic and social support they need to achieve.

Researchers have advocated for several more components to be put in place for literacy programs to be successful with students with LEP. These components include the following:

1. Meaningful literature that relates to the sociocultural backgrounds of students (Figueroa, Fradd, & Correa, 1989; Goldenberg, Reese, & Gallimore, 1992; Poplin & Phillips, 1993; Ruiz, 1989).
2. Opportunities for students to make their own meaning of new knowledge by relating it to their existing knowledge (Figueroa et al., 1989; Gersten & Jimenez, 1994; Tuyay, Jennings, & Dixon, 1993).
3. Instruction that responds to present abilities and strengths of students, slowly challenging them to learn new information and take more risks (Gersten & Jimenez, 1994; Goldman & Rueda, 1988).
4. The integration rather than fragmentation of curricular components (Ruiz, 1989).
5. The building of a literate community of learners wherein teachers and students construct meaning together (Edwards & Mercer, 1987; Goodman & Goodman, 1990; Tuyay et al., 1993; Wells, Chang, & Maher, 1990).

The case study presented in this article describes an excellent example of a program that can be successful with students with LEP even though native language support is not available. The participants are a fourth-grade Vietnamese-speaking boy, his special education teacher, and his classmates. The classroom is part of the Early Literacy Project (ELP). ELP was originally designed for students with learning disabilities, but the theoretical principles are closely matched with those identified by researchers as being beneficial for students with LEP. A brief description of the project's principles and activities is provided in Figure 1. Readers are directed to Englert, Raphael, and Mariage (1994) for more in-depth reading on the ELP.

This study was conducted in a special education classroom—the only type of setting in which ELP is presently in place. However, the features of ELP that benefit students with LEP could be incorporated into any general or bilingual education classroom. The original purpose of this study was to answer the following research questions:

1. Which aspects, if any, of the Early Literacy Project context support the language acquisition and literacy development of a student with LEP?
2. How do the special education teacher and students engage the student with LEP and promote his or her membership in the ELP community?
3. What is the nature of the student's participation in the ELP context, and what scaffolds does the teacher provide to further the student's participation and development?
4. What is the nature of gains, if any, in reading and writing achievement over time in the ELP context?

FIGURE 1
ELP Principles and Activities

Principles of the Early Literacy Project
- Teaching to Self-Regulation
- Responsive Instruction
- Building Literate Communities
- Literacy in Meaningful Activities
- An Integrated Curriculum

Morning Message

Description: Students dictate experience stories. Teacher acts as scribe in recording ideas, and as coach in modeling, guiding, and prompting literacy strategies.

Purposes: To model and conventionalize writing and self-monitoring strategies; to demonstrate writing conventions; to provide additional reading and comprehension experiences; to make connections between oral and written texts; to promote sense of community; to empower students; to provide meaningful and purposeful contexts for literacy strategies.

Thematic Unit

Description: Teacher and students brainstorm, organize, write drafts, read texts, or interview people to get additional information about a topic or theme from multiple sources, and use reading/writing strategies flexibly to develop and communicate their knowledge. Oral/written literacy connections are made apparent.

Purposes: To model taught learning (lead Author's Center and other activities); to introduce literacy language, genres, and strategies; to model reading/writing processes and connections; to provide interrelated and meaningful contexts for the acquisition and application of literacy knowledge; to conventionalize and develop shared knowledge about the purpose, meaning, and self-regulation of literacy acts.

Author's Center

Description: Process writing approach (students plan, organize, draft, edit texts). Students partner, write, and work collaboratively to brainstorm ideas, gather additional information, write drafts, share their drafts, receive questions, and write final draft.

Purposes: To develop a sense of community; to develop shared knowledge; to provide opportunities for students to rehearse literacy strategies; to empower students in the appropriation and transformation of strategies.

Literature Response

Description: Students read stories and respond to those stories in various ways (e.g., sequence stories, illustrate story events, map story events or story structure, summarize story, etc.)

Purposes: To promote students' application of literacy strategies; to present varied genres to students; to promote students' ownership of the discourse about texts; to further students' enjoyment of texts; to make text structures visible to students.

Author's Chair

Description: Students read books, poems, personal writing. Students control discourse and support each other. Students ask questions, answer questions, and act as informants to peers and teacher.

Purposes: To promote reading/writing connection; to empower students as members of the community; to allow students to make public their literacy knowledge and performance; to develop shared knowledge.

Unstructured Silent Reading

Description: Independent reading; reading to an adult; listening to new story at listening center.

Purposes: To work on fluency for author's chair; to provide experience with varied genres.

Partner Reading/Writing

Description: Choral reading and taped story reading. Partner reading and partner writing.

Purposes: To provide opportunities for students to fluently read and write connected texts; to provide opportunities for students to use literacy language and knowledge; to develop reading/writing vocabulary and enjoyment of reading.

It is recognized that the ELP program may not be ideal for all students with LEP, and not all such students will meet the same degree of success as the student studied here. This study does not negate the importance of emphasizing the native languages of students with LEP as part of successful literacy programs. Rather, it adds to the research a case example of how an instructional program's implementation provided one such student with a positive, supportive learning environment. According to Walton (1992), single case studies such as this one will "provide at least one anchor that steadies the ship of generalization until more anchors can be fixed for eventual boarding" (p. 19).

METHODS

Design

In this single case study, one student with LEP is studied from one school year to the next. Although this one example may not be powerful enough to generalize scientifically to all cases of students with LEP, it can be used to reinforce research in the area. Lincoln and Guba (1985) stated that "the case study is a fitting capstone to the *continuous* reporting process that characterizes naturalistic inquiry—the culmination and codification of myriad formal and informal reports that have gone before" (p. 358).

Participants

Ranh. The student in this study, Ranh, is a 12-year-old boy from Vietnam. He came to the United States with his parents and several siblings about 3 years prior to the study (at age 9). The primary language of Ranh and his family is Vietnamese, and they speak little English.

When Ranh came to the United States, he was in the second grade. Ranh spent one half day at the Bilingual Instructional Center (BIC) at Winter Elementary School and one half day in a general education classroom at his local school, Park Elementary. In the third grade, Ranh was classified as having a learning disability, according to state guidelines, with evaluations being conducted through the use of an interpreter. He continued to spend part of the

day at BIC, but the remainder of the day was split between the general education and special education classrooms at Park Elementary School. The special education placement, Tara's ELP classroom, was the setting of this study. Ranh spent one half day in a general education classroom and one half day in Tara's special education resource classroom. He no longer attended BIC, based on Tara's request to have him spend more time in her classroom.

An issue to be addressed here is whether Ranh was correctly classified as an exceptional student or whether his lack of academic progress was due solely to his cultural and linguistic difference. This issue was discussed in conversations with Tara after she had been working with Ranh for nearly 3 years. Her feelings were that his cultural and linguistic differences accounted for some of his lack of progress, but they were not the primary cause. She felt that he had a true learning disability as well. There is no evidence that Ranh could read or write in Vietnamese or that he was learning to do so at home or in BIC. In addition, the difficulties he experienced in learning were unique. They differed from difficulties Tara had witnessed with other Vietnamese-speaking students she had taught. Results of evaluations, combined with accounts of day-to-day classroom experiences by his teacher, led the researcher to believe that Ranh did indeed have a learning disability as well as limited English proficiency.

At one point, school personnel who had worked with Ranh suggested that he should be considered for a classification of having an emotional impairment. Tara spoke out against this. She explained that his aggression and negative behavior were due to his frustration over not understanding the language and culture surrounding him, and not because he had an emotional impairment.

Tara. Tara has been teaching special education at Park Elementary School for 6 years. She is certified in special education and deaf education. She speaks only English and does not have any training in bilingual education. Ranh was placed on Tara's caseload in the third grade, when he came to her classroom for part of the day. When Ranh began fourth grade, she asked that he be placed in her classroom for half the day, rather than go to BIC. She felt this arrangement would be more beneficial to him both academically and socially. This was agreed upon by other members of the special education placement committee.

Ranh's Classmates. When the study began, there were 14 students in the special education classroom: 9 boys (including Ranh) and 5 girls, from fourth to sixth grade. Of these students, 12 were classified as having learning disabilities, 1 as having educable mental retardation, and 1 as having emotional impairments. The students went to one of three different general education classrooms when they were not in Tara's classroom. Most of the students were in Tara's room about half of the day. The ethnic backgrounds of the students were as follows: 50% Caucasian (12 students), 21% African American (5 students), 25% Hispanic American (6 students), and 4% Asian (1 student, Ranh).

Toward the end of the study, Tara's class combined with another resource class. After the classes were combined, there were 2 teachers and 24 students: 14 boys and 10 girls. The grade levels and disability classifications of the incoming students were similar to those of Tara's original students.

Setting

Park Elementary School is a public school in a midwestern city. It was one of several schools with teachers involved in the 4-year Early Literacy Project. Tara participated in the project for all 4 years, so her teaching is deeply rooted in the ELP curriculum.

Of the activities listed in Figure 1, Tara's class does Morning Message, Journal Writing, and Author's Chair on a daily basis. Partner Reading and Unstructured Silent Reading are done every other day, on an alternating basis. Tara's class is always involved in a Thematic Unit, each unit spanning about 3 weeks. The students do modified versions of Author's Center and Literature Response, working independently or in pairs, rather than in groups, to write their own stories and reactions to literature.

Data Collection

The purpose of this study was to compare Ranh's performance in the classroom from the 1992–1993 school year to the 1993–1994 school year to determine whether the ELP setting was beneficial to his literacy development and language acquisition. Data concerning Ranh for 1992–1993 were gathered retroactively from Tara, and new data for 1993–1994 were collected during the spring of 1994.

Tara was contacted on April 4, 1994, with details of the proposed study. At this time, parent permission slips and video release forms were distributed to allow all students in Tara's classroom to be observed and videotaped. Next, the following items from 1992–1993 were obtained: a sample of Ranh's journal; two videotapes of Ranh dictating a Morning Message; the chart paper from four of Ranh's Morning Messages (not the same as those in the videotapes); a sample writing exercise in which Ranh was asked to write an individual Morning Message; and Ranh's scores on four reading and writing test measures used in the ELP (Writing Vocabulary, Sentence Dictation, Written Recall, and Explanation). These measures are described in Figure 2.

The collection of new data began in Tara's classroom on April 22, 1994. The classroom was visited as much as possible on Mondays, Wednesdays, and Fridays until the end of the school year. (Data could not be collected on Tuesdays or Thursdays due to the researcher's own class schedule.) There were several days when Ranh was not in school. Although absenteeism was not usually a problem with Ranh, he missed an average of 1 day each week during this time for family vacations, illnesses, and once for an injury sustained on the school playground.

Data gathered during the spring of 1994 consisted of the following: approximately 12 hours of videotape of classroom activities; a sample of writing by Ranh and two other boys in his reading group; a sample from Ranh's journal; an audiotaped interview with Ranh; an audiotaped interview with Tara; and scores for six reading and writing test measures used in ELP (SORT, Durrell, Writing Vocabulary, Sentence Dictation, Written Recall, and Explanation).

FIGURE 2
ELP Reading and Writing Test Measures

Slosson Oral Reading Test (SORT)

The SORT is an individually administered test of the student's ability to read words correctly. The words are grouped into sets of 20, each list progressing up one reading level in difficulty. A raw score, total number of words read correctly at all levels, is converted into a grade level equivalent score.

Durrell

The Durrell is an individually administered test of the student's ability to read a passage and recall the content. The Administrator records exactly how the student reads the words in each passage, the time it takes to read it, and how many chunks of information the student remembers. The percentages are given for each reading level.

Writing Vocabulary

This measure is group administered and timed. Each student is given 10 minutes to write a random list of all the words he or she knows. The students are prompted with suggestions, such as "What do you like to eat?" The number of words attempted is compared with the number of words written correctly.

Sentence Dictation

This measure is group administered. The administrator reads a sentence, then repeats it slowly so that each word is somewhat isolated. Each student is asked to write the sentence as it is read. One point is given for each phoneme written correctly.

Written Recall

This group-administered measure begins with the administrator reading a passage aloud as each student follows along with his or her own copy. Then, without the text, each student is asked to write as much as he or she can remember about the passage. The measure is scored according to the number of main ideas and chunks of information remembered, organization, and the amount of relevant information remembered. Scores are reported as an overall holistic score and a primary trait score.

Expert Writing Measure

In this group-administered measure, each student is asked to write a topic on which he or she is an expert. The students may choose their own topics. The measure is scored on the number of ideas presented, organization, author's voice, level of interest to the reader, and readability. Scores are reported as an overall holistic score, a primary trait score, and a reader sensitivity score.

Explanation Writing Measure

Similar to the Expert Writing Measure, this measure asks each student to explain something to someone else in writing. The measure is scored on the number of steps, organization, audience targeted, author's voice, level of interest to the reader, and readability. Scores are reported as an overall holistic score, a primary trait score, and a reader sensitivity score.

Data Analysis

Videotapes. The two 1992–1993 videotapes and the several hours of spring 1994 videotapes were transcribed and read thoroughly. Each transcript was reread, and examples that would help to answer the original four research questions were noted. The transcriptions were then analyzed for interactions involving Ranh. An interaction was defined by the researcher as a set of verbalizations by two or more people about a particular topic. For example, if a student asks a question, the conversation that follows among teachers and students until the question is answered is considered one interaction. The start of a new topic indicated a new interaction. Several items were noted: the date and type of the activity in which the interactions occurred; the total number of interactions involving Ranh during the activity; the number of interactions initiated by Ranh; the number of interactions involving Ranh but initiated by others; the number of turns in each interaction (distinguishing between Ranh's and others' turns); and the number of words spoken in each interaction (distinguishing between the number spoken by Ranh and by others). Figure 3 shows a chart designed to record this information.

Finally, the videotape transcriptions were studied twice more. First, fidgety or shy behaviors (e.g., hanging off his chair, making noises, or wearing his hood in class) were noted. Second, instances were noted when Ranh asked for clarification, corrected himself, or contributed to the group although he appeared not to be paying attention.

The extensive analysis of the videotapes showed how Ranh's language skills, social interactions, and behavior changed over time. These are as important to note in studying his performance in the classroom as are the scores on test measures and changes in written work.

Test Measures. Previously established guidelines were followed in scoring all of the ELP test measures administered to Ranh. The scores for all pre- and posttest measures were charted and the results recorded in Figure 4.

Interviews. The teacher and student interviews were also analyzed for examples that might shed light on answers to the research questions. Careful attention was paid to any mention of Ranh's background, in attempts to gain as much insight into this area as possible.

The student interview was analyzed a second time with regard to the student's interaction with the interviewer. Noted were: (1) the total number of interactions involving Ranh during the interview; (2) the number of interactions initiated by Ranh; (3) the number of interactions initiated by the interviewer; (4) the number of turns in each interaction (distinguishing between Ranh's and the interviewer's turns); and (5) the number of words spoken in each interaction (distinguishing between the number spoken by Ranh and the number spoken by the interviewer). Finally, the student interview was examined a third time for the number of instances when Ranh asked for clarification and when he corrected himself for better communication with the interviewer.

Student Writing Samples. Ranh's writing samples were collected and analyzed to determine use of new vocabulary words, organization of ideas, and inventive spelling of words. This information was useful in determining the extent to which Ranh took risks in his writing and attempted to use language that may have been new to him.

RESULTS

Ranh demonstrated varied levels of improvement in the areas of behavior, academics, verbal skills, and social relationships with others.

Improvements in Ranh's Behavior

The most marked area of improvement for Ranh was his behavior. Many teachers at Park Elementary School were familiar with his inappropriate behavior. Tara described it like this:

> He had a reputation, and everyone would come to me and say, "You need to put him away. He is a crazy kid." I mean, you wouldn't believe all the sad things they have said about Ranh . . . . I just bite my tongue, because you can't convince someone who hasn't been through it with him . . . . Yet, I look at him and think he's come so far.

Tara felt that he was not often given the time and attention he needed. She thought he must

FIGURE 3
Student Interaction

Date/Type of Document	Total Number of Interactions	Number Initiated by Ranh	Number Initiated by Others (Name)	Number of Turns (Ranh/Others)	Number of Words (Ranh/Others)

Average Number of Words per Turn   = _____

Average Number of Words per Interaction   = _____

Average Number of Turns per Interactions   = _____

Percentage of Interactions Initiated by Ranh = _____

FIGURE 4
ELP Test Scores

Test Measure	Pretest Scores (Spring 1993)	Posttest Scores (Spring 1994)	Results
Slosson Oral Reading Test (SORT)	Test not given due to student's low reading ability at this time.	Raw Score: 6 words Grade Equivalent: 0.3	Gain of 0.3 grade levels.
Durrel	Test not given due to student's low reading ability at this time.	Level 1A: 83% reading accuracy. 17% comprehension Level 1B: 50% reading accuracy. 0% comprehension	1A = Ability level 1B = Frustration level
Writing Vocabulary	24 words attempted/14 correct 10 minutes time. Average of 2.4 words/minute attempted. Average of 1.4 words/minute correct.	22 words attempted/12 correct 5 minutes time. Average of 3.6 words/minute attempted. Average of 2.0 words/minute correct.	Average gain of: 1.2 words/minute attempted 0.6 words/minute correct.
Sentence Dictation	1 out of 37 phonemes written correctly.	24 out of 37 phonemes written correctly.	Gain of 23 phonemes (62.2%) written correctly.
Written Recall	Holistic score: 0 Primary trait score: 1	Holistic score: 0 Primary trait score: 1	No gain.
Explanation Writing Measure	Holistic score: 1 Primary trait score: 5 Reader sensitivity: 1	Holistic score: 2 Primary trait score: 6 Reader sensitivity: 2	Improvement in all scoring areas.

have been frustrated and angry at not knowing what to do or how to talk to people. This frustration came out in the form of aggressive behaviors. Tara began to help him deal with these frustrations and control his behaviors as soon as he came to her classroom as a student:

> When he came into my room, immediately the rules went into place and he knew what to expect and he was always getting into trouble. All day long I'd hear myself saying, "Ranh, Ranh," and giving him the look, but normally that's all it takes and then 5 minutes later he's back to doing something else. But it's not out of control like he was in the beginning, outside of my classroom.

He began to see Tara as a person he could trust when he became frustrated. She would be there to pay him the much-needed attention rather than to scold him. A milestone in his development and relationship with Tara occurred in third grade:

> At the very beginning of the year, when he was in BIC, he was getting into trouble every day. I sat down with him and I started talking to him and he started bawling . . . . First of all, I had never seen him with any kind of feeling whatsoever except for anger and goofiness, not even happy, just silly. But he just started bawling, and I knew it was because he was frustrated. He could only get out a little bit of it and he wasn't understanding, and that's when I knew he was coming . . . . I hate to say it, but it really was a turning point, and I felt like it was a breakthrough, because he never did that before.

In addition to his behavioral and emotional gains, Ranh made progress in his literacy development as well, as indicated in the following sections.

Which Aspects of the Early Literacy Project Context Support the Language Acquisition and Literacy Development of the Student with LEP?

Judging by the data collected and the observations made of Ranh in Tara's classroom, the aspects that supported Ranh most in his achievement are the many opportunities for extended dialogue, the small-group or partner activities, and the consistency present in the classroom.

The context of Tara's ELP classroom provided opportunities for students to communicate almost constantly. In fact, the only time when silence was required in Tara's room was for 5 minutes when students wrote in their journals. Tara talked about the constant dialogue:

> He learned language from the kids, because that's all it is in ELP. It's the kids' language. So he's picking up on all their language, and some of them [don't] speak grammatically correctly, and he [picks] up on that too. But, I mean, that's what he needs to learn. He doesn't need to learn things from a book that teaches present tense and past tense . . . . He needs to learn language like little kids do when they're growing up . . . . They learn it by hearing it . . . . He just needs a ton of language, just everyday language.

Smaller groups, and especially one-on-one situations with Tara, seemed to be most beneficial for Ranh. Small-group activities gave Ranh an opportunity to interact with his peers without the bombardment of several people talking at once (e.g., as in large-group activities such as Morning Message). This was observed on May 10, 1994, during the first Morning Message activity that Tara's students did as a large group with the other special education students who joined their class. Ranh was chosen to lead the activity, but he declined. As the activity began and students started yelling out suggestions and questions, Ranh sat backward in his chair and stuck his head under the jacket that was hanging on the back of the chair. During the student interview, Ranh explained why he didn't prefer this large-group activity:

Interviewer:	What else is hard?
Ranh:	Morning Message.
Interviewer:	Morning Message is hard?
Ranh:	Yeah.
Interviewer:	What's hard about that?
Ranh:	They yell, they say, "Go play! Go play!" They yell that. Make me crazy.
Interviewer:	When too many people yell at once?
Ranh:	Yeah.

Ranh also seemed much more willing to take risks in smaller groups, when the pressure of performing in front of others was lessened.

The following excerpt is taken from a reading lesson about the rain forest with Tara. They were studying a poster of animals found in the rain forest. During this lesson, Ranh sat up in his chair, leaning forward, interacting enthusiastically, and even joking with Tara:

Tara:	Do you think the jaguar would like to eat the butterfly?
Ranh:	No!
Tara:	Why not?
Ranh:	Because it's too little.
Tara:	Yeah. It's too little.
Ranh:	Eat him (pointing to another picture).
Tara:	Yeah, it would probably like him. I don't know if this is a jaguar or a leopard.
Ranh:	Leopard!
Tara:	What is that (pointing to the word by the picture)? A jaguar or a leopard?
Ranh:	A leopard. A jaguar!
Tara:	A jaguar. Okay, how many points do you think you should get? (Tara awards up to three points per lesson to each student toward his or her individual behavior goals.)
Ranh:	Five (giggling).
Tara:	How many points can you get?
Ranh:	Three.

Other small groups or partner activities occurred when students worked quietly together on tasks that piqued their interests. They chose their own books to read, chose their own topics for writing assignments, or worked together to find their own solutions to problems. Dialogue took place constantly in these groups, with students guiding each other and furthering each other's learning. When an activity consisted of one student and Tara, the relationship was similar. The student and Tara worked together to construct knowledge and solve problems.

Large-group activities in Tara's class were not usually teacher directed. The students often governed how the activities took shape and progressed. Dialogue occurred constantly, with students adding to the discussion at all times. Often the room became noisy, but it was purposeful noise directed at completing the activi-

ty as a group. Although Ranh was somewhat intimidated by larger groups, there were still times when he participated. Once when Tara was taking suggestions for a concluding sentence for a Morning Message story, Ranh's hand went straight up. He suggested, "Laura had a fun." Although his English was not yet perfect, he had become confident enough to practice what he knew and add his ideas to a class discussion.

Finally, Ranh benefited a great deal from the consistency Tara showed when explaining concepts, giving directions, asking questions, and enforcing rules. This helped Ranh rely on her to let him know what to expect. Ranh even came to regulate his own behaviors and consequences. One day, as Tara readied the class for a choral reading activity, Ranh asked to read at his desk instead. Tara asked him what the consequence was for taking that unearned privilege. Ranh responded that the consequence was five points taken off his reward points for the day (a system used with the whole class). Tara left the final decision up to Ranh. After considering the situation, Ranh decided to participate.

Tara explained the situation in her classroom:

> I tried to put myself in his position and think about, you know, if I went to a country and didn't speak their language, and there's 10 different adults telling me 10 different things, none of which I understand . . . . You're just going to wish for one person to say the same thing to you over and over again so you know what they want.
>
> [H]e knows that I'm consistent, and if I say I'm going to do something, I do it. So he knows what the boundaries are, and he knows if he crosses them, he can tell me exactly what's going to happen . . . . If he throws something, I'll say, "What should happen?" He says, "Five points."

How Do the Special Education Teacher and Students Engage the Student with LEP and Promote His Membership into the ELP Community?

The principles and beliefs underlying ELP provide for the building of strong classroom communities. Everyone is seen for his or her strengths and interests. Each student has the opportunity to be an expert and a leader, two roles usually reserved for the teacher. Accordingly, in these communities, the teacher takes on the role of learner. Each person is made to feel welcome, comfortable, safe, and above all, respected. There was a particularly strong feeling of community in Tara's classroom.

There were many instances when Tara and the other students engaged Ranh in discussions, and Tara was always conscious of the degree to which Ranh was involved. If he seemed to be tuning out because he did not understand or felt shy, she attempted to bring him back in. The other students actively kept him involved and praised his efforts. One example occurred when Amy recognized his contribution during a Morning Message activity. The group was editing a particularly long sentence, trying to decide on the proper punctuation. Tara asked the students to reread the sentence so she could point out where they paused, requiring a comma.

Tara (to group):	What did you just do here? You stopped.
Ranh:	Comma.
Tara:	Good Ranh. Comma.
Amy:	He should get a point for that, Ms. W.
Many students:	Good Ranh.
Student:	Everybody puts a comma when you stop.
Amy:	Yeah, but Ranh did good.

Another example of drawing Ranh into the classroom community centered around a special birthday party Tara arranged for him:

[Y]ou could tell he was excited about it and the other kids were very accepting . . . you know, I don't do that for everybody, but I talked to them and I told them. Ranh wasn't in the room, and I just told them that they don't celebrate in Vietnam and . . . I want him to know that we think he's special and we think that it's special that he celebrates this day.

Tara also recognized the need for Ranh to find a place in her classroom by expressing his language and customs. At first Ranh did not seem to want to share his different background with others. Tara recounted an instance when the school janitor, also from Vietnam, greeted Ranh in Vietnamese. Ranh responded briefly under his breath and walked away. When Tara asked what the janitor had said, Ranh did not respond.

Later, after Ranh realized that his interests and traditions were welcome in Tara's classroom, he was much more willing to share his background with others. Tara's respect for his interest in karate is symbolic of this feeling of acceptance. While other teachers punished Ranh's imitation of karate moves, even on the playground, Tara allowed Ranh to practice them when appropriate. She asked him about karate and his grandfather, who practices karate in Vietnam. She also had him do writing assignments on the topic.

What Is the Nature of the Participation of the Student with LEP in the ELP Context and What Scaffolds Does the Special Education Teacher Provide to Further the Student's Participation and Development?

The nature of Ranh's participation changed a great deal from one year to the next. The first videotapes of him during Morning Message showed a shy, withdrawn student who interacted only minimally with others. Ranh did not contribute to the activity unless asked a specific question by Tara or another student. Most often it was Tara who directly elicited a response from him. Then his responses were very brief, usually consisting of a "yes" or "no." He also tended to physically shy away from the others, sinking into his chair or turning away.

Tara described Ranh's initial participation in Author's Chair as minimal. He would sit in the back of the group, listening but not asking questions. He often declined his turn in the chair. In contrast, a year later he participated openly during an Author's Chair activity. In this excerpt from May 18, 1994, Richard is in the chair, already having read his journal entry. Ranh is sitting in the middle of the group toward the front with his hand up:

Richard:	Ranh.
Ranh:	Why you go to his house?
Richard:	(Looks at Tara.)
Tara:	Did you say why?
Ranh:	Yeah.

Richard:	I don't know. (He looks around for more questions and Ranh raises his hand again.) Ranh.
Ranh:	What you do at your dad's house?
Richard:	Huh?
Ranh:	What you do at your dad's house?
Richard:	Nothing (shrugging).

Ranh is not daunted when students do not understand at first, as he may have been at one time. Rather, he repeats himself and continues to participate.

Ranh's participation progressed in other activities to the point where he voluntarily contributed ideas and opinions to group discussion, asked questions when he didn't understand something or wanted more information, and initiated conversation with peers and adults. One example of this is when he asked for clarification during the student interview:

Interviewer:	When you are in Miss White's class, what are you expected to do in a group with other kids?
Ranh:	What mean?
Interviewer:	When you're in a group, when you're working with other kids, what are you supposed to do? What should you do?
Ranh:	Tell them, tell them how to work.

Tara commented about this in the teacher interview:

Ranh is learning to defend himself, you know, verbally. He's telling people he doesn't understand and asking them to show him what they're talking about, and he's finally got enough language. He feels that he can communicate with the kids and actually be a participant in any of the groups that we have.

This year in fourth grade, I was amazed. It was probably the second week when we were doing Author's Chair. He raised his hand and I thought he was going to ask a question. He turned to me when she called on him and said, "What she talk about?" Instead of me saying, "Do you understand what we're doing?" he started coming out and saying, "I don't understand. Tell me what so I can participate."

This progress was not always easy and steady. Tara described the process of Ranh's slowly testing his ability to successfully contribute to class discussions:

Last year I had him in third grade . . . He didn't participate as much. I had to act out a lot and then he would participate . . . . He'd yell things out, you know, "Capital!" and if we were in the wrong place, it wasn't appropriate. But he was hearing those things and he knew that's what I was looking for. He'd yell, "Capital!" when that's not what we were working on, or "Period!" when we'd already got one. At the beginning it was very inappropriate . . . but he knew what the language was, and then it became more appropriate.

Tara was very conscious of Ranh's ever-changing abilities and needs. She was always there to provide him with help if he needed it, scaffolding his learning by building on his strengths and focusing on improving his weaknesses. Tara acted things out for Ranh when possible. This strategy, she said, stemmed from her background in deaf education. She also built upon one of Ranh's great strengths, his ability to draw. He had a special artistic talent. Tara began to capitalize on this strength from the very beginning. If they did not understand each other, they drew pictures and Tara provided the new vocabulary words for Ranh. An example occurred when Tara asked him about his injury on the playground. He had cut his lip, but not badly enough for stitches. When Tara asked whether he had ever had stitches, he told a story about cutting his arm while climbing on a "door." Seeing that his meaning was not understood, he got a piece of paper and pencil and drew a picket fence with a gate. Tara told him the word he wanted was "gate," not "door." He repeated the correct word a few times and then finished his story with the right vocabulary.

Tara was adept at catching him at critical moments when he was curious or slightly confused but not frustrated. If Ranh seemed to be fading out of a group because he did not understand, Tara would stop the group and take the time to explain to Ranh what they were discussing. She always used words he knew while introducing new ones, challenging him enough to keep his interest but without frustrating him.

An excellent example of this occurred during Laura's Morning Message on April 29, 1994:

Tara: Ranh, do you know what this means?

Amy: When you take a balloon, and like this . . . Shweeeeooooo (imitates the squeaking noise a balloon makes when you pull the lip tight as the air exhales)!

Tara: No, no, no. Ranh, do you know the balloons you buy in the store?

Ranh: Yeah.

Tara: Well, there's something people do that is . . . (looks at Laura) not good for you! You know this? They take off the tie on the balloon and put their mouth on it a little bit and they breathe in the balloon air. They go like . . . (sucks in). They breathe in the balloon air, and when they talk, their voice changes like this (using a very high voice). That's what she's talking about.

This example also shows how students played a role in scaffolding Ranh's understanding. While certain students, such as Amy, seemed to be more active in this role, all students were patient and understanding when lessons were halted. In fact, they often benefited from the explanations as well.

What Is the Nature of Gains, If Any, in Reading and Writing Achievement Over Time in the ELP Context?

The gains made by Ranh are varied across situations. As can be seen in Figure 4, the degree to which Ranh's test scores demonstrated gains varied from one measure to another. Ranh's oral reading ability indeed improved. In spring 1993, the two reading measures, SORT and Durrell, were not administered to him because he was unable to perform the tasks asked of him. One year later, in spring 1994, he was able to read at a minimum level. He scored at the 0.3 or primer grade level on the SORT and at the first-grade level on the Durrell. His reading level is still far below his present grade level

placement, but improvement has been seen. Ranh's comprehension of oral language improved substantially, as seen in the Sentence Dictation results. In spring 1993, he wrote only the first phoneme of the dictated sentence. One year later, he attempted the entire dictated sentence, with 24 of the 37 phonemes written correctly.

The Writing Vocabulary measure results were difficult to interpret. On the pretest, Ranh wrote for the entire time allotted—10 minutes. He listed 24 unrelated words, 14 of them spelled correctly. On the posttest, he stopped after 6 minutes and did not want to continue. He attempted 22 words, and 12 of them were correct. Ranh's score improved from 1.4 to 2.0 words correct per minute. Ranh's scores on the Written Recall measure were the same from one year to the next. His test papers looked much the same with one or two chunks of information recalled, neither of them relevant to the information in the passage. On both tests, Ranh dictated his ideas to the administrator.

Ranh's Explanation Paper improved slightly the second year. He had more steps in his explanation, using key words such as "first," and "after that." On both tests, he dictated his explanation to the researcher. His thoughts and oral communication abilities seemed to improve, but his ability to write them on his own did not.

Another source for studying Ranh's gains is samples of his journal entries. From one year to the next, little difference is seen in the topics of his writing. He stayed with the ideas of playing, going to play at a friend's house, or going to the store. His writing remained quite stilted, but he did use some new vocabulary. In spring 1994, he wrote the words "moak in trol (remote control)." Ranh did not wait to master the words before he risked using them. Instead, he used inventive spelling to try new words in his writing as he acquired them in his oral language.

An important point is that the interpretation of these test measures and journal entry samples does not begin to summarize the progress Ranh has made in his oral language acquisition. Observations in the classroom over a year's time show a student who became confident in his command of a second language. The breadth of his vocabulary expanded continually. There were still many words, phrases, and grammatical rules that he did not know, yet he took control of his learning enough to ask for clarification and new words in English. This was evidenced when he drew a picture of the gate for Tara.

The nature of Ranh's interactions in the Morning Message activity changed as well. He began to interact more often, for longer periods of time, initiating more interactions. On October 15, 1992, a Morning Message was videotaped in which Ranh was the leader. There were 19 interactions involving Ranh during this activity. Ranh averaged 1.59 words per turn and 3.42 words per interaction. He took an average of 2.16 turns per interaction and initiated only 10.53% of the interactions.

On April 29, 1994, a Morning Message activity was videotaped in which Ranh was *not* the leader. Even in a much less emphasized role, as part of the class audience, Ranh interacted a great deal more. During this activity, there were 11 interactions involving Ranh. He averaged 3.95 words per turn and 7.54 words per interaction. He took an average of 1.9 turns per interaction and initiated 63.6% of the interactions. These numbers indicate that Ranh is now initiating more interactions, rather than waiting to be asked a question. Also, he is saying more during his turns, rather than answering with a "yes" or "no."

DISCUSSION

Over all, Ranh improved most in his acquisition of oral language and his confidence in interacting in a second language. He still had some difficulty with his reading and writing skills. This might have been due to a combination of three different factors: (1) the setbacks Ranh had due to his negative behavior in previous years; (2) the fact that Ranh did not learn to read or write in Vietnamese before learning a second language; and (3) the fact that Ranh probably does have a true learning disability as well as limited English proficiency, as Tara believes he does.

Despite the many obstacles that Ranh has had to face in the past and those he will continue to face in the future, the ELP learning environment fostered his development substantially. Other students with LEP could benefit from many features of this classroom structure. One is the idea of smaller grouping to increase opportunities to communicate with peers and decrease the stress of larger groups. A second is the idea of building classroom communities where everyone feels safe, comfortable, and respected for his or her strengths and diversity. A third is the constant opportunity to use language in different situations with different people.

Of course, this case study does not predict equal success for all students with LEP. There are aspects of this particular situation that cannot be generalized to other settings. The most important one is the relationship that existed between Tara and Ranh. The amount of one-to-one attention Ranh received and the sincere, caring, trustful bond he shared with his teacher are not easily replicated.

The key to establishing such a relationship is a foundation built on mutual respect. Ranh respected the fact that Tara set consistent goals for her students and for herself. Tara respected the fact that Ranh was from a different background and needed extra support to be successful. She began to incorporate his culture and language into the classroom activities, but not as much as she would have liked. Nonetheless, Ranh went from being almost ashamed of his different background, as seen in the instance with the janitor, to wanting to share it with the class. He taught his classmates words in Vietnamese, drew pictures of Vietnamese buildings and people, and completed a project on Vietnam for a school multicultural fair.

Although this environment was beneficial without utilizing Ranh's native language, that is an aspect that cannot be ignored. Whenever possible, it is important to support students with LEP in their native language and to incorporate their cultures into the classroom. There is a need for more qualified teachers with backgrounds in bilingual education as well as teachers who fluently speak languages other than English. However, until this happens, principles and activities such as those employed in the Early Literacy Project curriculum may provide the needed support for students with LEP in a variety of classroom settings.

RESEARCH LIMITATIONS

One limitation to this study is that it was conducted by one researcher. While all information is accurate, data analysis and interpretations were formed by one person, making interrater reliability impossible.

A second limitation, the lack of information about Ranh's schooling in Vietnam, his language and literacy abilities in Vietnamese, and his experiences outside of school, leaves some spaces in the data. Due to this lack of information, the researcher was sometimes left to rely on interpretations and stories recounted by Tara.

Tara's experience was unique, due in great part to the fact that she is unique as a teacher. Her patience, perseverance, and respect for students is not the case for all teachers in all settings. While the principles and activities of ELP can be replicated in any classroom with any teacher, and even with any academic subject, Tara's characteristics cannot. Therefore, the degree to which this study can be replicated may depend on the personal characteristics of the teacher. Thus, the issue of generalizability is a third limitation to the study.

Finally, the researcher began this study during Ranh's second year in the ELP classroom with Tara. Although data were collected by another researcher during Ranh's first year, no systematic data were collected before he entered the ELP program. For this study, Ranh's performance during his first year in ELP was used as a baseline and compared to his performance during his second year. There was no baseline of performance established prior to his enrollment in ELP, other than information recounted by Tara. Also, Ranh is no longer enrolled in ELP. His family moved away, and he was enrolled in fifth grade in another district. There is no available information on his performance now that he is no longer in an ELP classroom. This study could be enhanced if systematic data had been collected before and after Ranh was enrolled in ELP.

REFERENCES

Chiang, R. A. (1994). Home-school communication for Asian students with limited English proficiency. *Kappa Delta Pi Record, 30*, 159–163.

Cummins, J. (1989). A theoretical framework for bilingual special education. *Exceptional Children, 56*, 111–119.

Cushner, K., McClelland, A., & Safford, P. (1992). *Human diversity in education: An integrative approach.* New York: McGraw-Hill.

Edwards, D., & Mercer, N. (1987). *Common knowledge: The development of understanding in the classroom.* London: Methuen.

Englert, C. S., Raphael, T. E., & Mariage, T. (1994). Developing a school-based discourse for literacy learning: A principled search for understanding. *Learning Disability Quarterly, 17*, 2–32.

Figueroa, R. A., Fradd, S. H., & Correa, V. I. (1989). Bilingual education and this special issue. *Exceptional Children, 56*, 174–178.

Fix, M., & Zimmerman, W. (1993). *Educating immigrant children: Chapter 1 in the changing city.* Washington DC: The Urban Institute Press.

Fradd, S. H., & Correa, V. I. (1989). Hispanic students at risk: Do we abdicate or advocate? *Exceptional Children, 56*, 105–110.

Gersten, R., & Jimenez, R. T. (1994). A delicate balance: Enhancing literature instruction for students of English as a second language. *The Reading Teacher, 47*, 438–449.

Gersten, R., & Woodward, J. (1994). The language-minority student and special education: Issues, trends, and paradoxes. *Exceptional Children, 60*, 310–322.

Goldenberg, C. (1992, April). *Promoting early literacy development among Spanish-speaking children: Lessons from two studies.* Paper presented at the annual meeting of the American Educational Research Association, San Francisco, CA.

Goldenberg, C., Reese, L., & Gallimore, R. (1992). Effects of literacy materials from school on Latino children's home experiences and early reading achievement. *American Journal of Education, 100*, 497–536.

Goldman, S., & Rueda, R. (1988). Developing writing skills in bilingual exceptional children. *Exceptional Children, 54*, 543–551.

Goodman, Y. M., & Goodman, K. S. (1990). Vygotsky in a whole-language perspective. In L. C. Moll (Ed.), *Vygotsky and education: Instructional implications and applications of sociohistorical psychology* (pp. 223–250). Cambridge, U.K.: Cambridge University Press.

Leo, J. (1994, November 7). Bilingualism: Que Pasa? *U.S.News & World Report*, p. 22.

Lincoln, Y. S., & Guba, E. G. (1985). *Naturalistic inquiry.* London: Sage.

McCollum, P. (1991). Cross-cultural perspectives on classroom discourse and literacy. In E. H. Hiebert (Ed.), *Literacy for a diverse society* (pp. 108–121). New York: Teachers College, Columbia University.

McKeon, D. (1994). When meeting "common" standards is uncommonly difficult. *Education Leadership, 51*, pp. 45–49.

Miramontes, O. B., & Commins, N. L. (1991). Redefining literacy and literacy contexts: Discovering a community of learners. In E. H. Hiebert (Ed.), *Literacy for a diverse society* (pp. 75–89). New York: Teachers College, Columbia University.

Poplin, M., & Phillips, L. (1993). Sociocultural aspects of language and literacy: Issues facing educators of students with learning disabilities. *Learning Disability Quarterly, 16*, 245–255.

Ruiz, N. T. (1989). An optimal learning environment for Rosemary. *Exceptional Children, 56*, 130–144.

Stein, C. B., Jr. (1986). *Sink or swim: The politics of bilingual education.* New York: Praeger.

Tuyay, S., Jennings, L., & Dixon, C. (1993, December). *Classroom discourse and opportunities to learn: An ethnographic study of knowledge construction in a bilingual third-grade classroom.* Paper presented at the annual meeting of the National Reading Conference, Charleston, SC.

Walton, J. (1992). Making the theoretical case. In C. Ragin & H. Becker (Eds.), *What is a case? The foundations of social inquiry* (pp. 121–137). Cambridge, U.K.: Cambridge University Press.

Wells, G., Chang, G. L. M., & Maher, A. (1990). Creating classroom communities of literate thinkers. In S. Sharan (Ed.), *Cooperative learning: Theory and research.* New York: Praeger.

ABOUT THE AUTHOR

WHITNEY HOSMER RAPP, Ph.D., is a former classroom teacher who recently completed her doctoral degree, Michigan State University.

Note: The names of all people and places mentioned in this article were changed to ensure confidentiality. I would like to thank Dr. Carol Sue Englert and Dr. Stanley Trent of Michigan State University for their guidance and advice on this study. Also, I would especially like to thank the participants of this study for their time, patience, and the many things they taught me about teaching and learning.

Making Connections: Developing Strategies to Teach African-American Gifted Learners Effectively

JOY L. BAYTOPS

Virginia Department of Education

DENNIS REED

Richmond Community High School

In classrooms all across the United States are young African Americans who respond to their environment in unique ways. According to some theorists, these students are often characterized as being more inquisitive than most of their age peers, they are better at discerning discrepancies and dealing with ambiguities, they are able to see unusual and remote associations, and they tend to be more intellectually playful (Clark, 1988). In some academic environments, these students would be labeled as "gifted." According to a recent report by the United States Department Of Education, states generally identify 3% to 5% of their school-aged population as gifted and talented (U.S. Department of Education, 1988). As gifted learners, these students have demonstrated achievement or potential for achievement that requires a specifically designed instructional program to meet their cognitive, creative, and affective needs.

While giftedness manifests itself across demographic groups in similar ways (Clark, 1988), research has also documented evidence of the unique and varied ways that gifted African-American learners display their strengths (Dabney, 1977; Hale-Benson, 1986; Hilliard, 1976; Shade, 1990). This article discusses the diverse characteristics of African-American gifted learners and provides a ratio-nale for designing specific instructional programs to meet their needs. One example of a classroom of African-American gifted students is described to shed some light on the uniqueness of student traits and instructional methodologies that best develop those traits.

RECOGNIZING GIFTEDNESS IN AFRICAN-AMERICAN STUDENTS

Why is it important that we focus specific attention on the gifts and talents of African-American learners? While African-American students make up approximately 25% of the school-aged population in the United States, they comprise less than half this proportion of students identified as gifted and served in public school programs across the country (Gallagher, 1995). Even with more widely used nontraditional assessment practices, these students remain underrepresented in gifted education programs nationwide. Consequently, they are denied access to educational experiences that could maximize their potential more effectively. On the other hand, their European American counterparts with similarly recognized gifts and talents receive special attention to enhance and nurture their potential across a variety of disciplines.

It has been only recently that educators have made efforts to delineate and characterize the particular strengths and learning needs of African-American gifted learners. Among the strengths identified are verbal fluency, creativity, wit, inventiveness, and aesthetic and spiritual sensitivity (Baldwin, 1989; Ford & Harris, 1991; Frasier, 1989; Hilliard, 1976; Patton & Baytops, 1995; Shade, 1990). Additionally, it has been noted that these students have learning preferences in the following intellectual, physiological, and social-emotional modes:

- Kinesthetic (i.e., expressive movement).
- Oral expression (reciting, singing, speaking).
- Interpersonal (preferring person-to-person contact over person-to-object).
- Field-dependent/relational (preferring experiences that are directly related to the context with which they are familiar) (Hale-Benson, 1986; Shade, 1990).

Although this research is formative and inclusive, it has led to the development of identification models and instructional methodologies that are multiple and varied. These new methodologies are supported by theoretical frameworks that have been created to identify and accentuate the strengths of these students in learning environments that provide for their cognitive, creative, and affective development (Patton & Baytops, 1995). However, we need to test these theories within the context of classrooms and determine how these constructs can be translated into practice.

CONNECTING STRENGTHS WITH CLASSROOM EXPERIENCES

To reduce the discrepancies that exist between the school and home environments of students, so-called constructivists recommend that an instructional framework be designed that closely aligns the learning experience with the sociocultural background of each student being served. According to socioconstructivists, learners interact with and interpret the world based on their own experiences (Peterson, 1996). Responsive classrooms are those in which the varied experiences of students are taken into account as they engage in learning activities (Peterson, 1996). Constructivists further recommend that peer group interaction be consistently fostered to influence the channeling of learning in the classroom (Fordham & Ogbu, 1986).

As with any other group with special needs, African-American gifted learners have particular needs that are met most effectively in specifically designed classes. An observer needs only to spend a brief period of time in a classroom with these students to witness the varying and unique manifestations of their gifts and talents. One such class is found in Richmond Community High School (RCHS), a secondary alternative school for gifted learners in Richmond, Virginia.

The Secondary School Experiential Learning Community project provided the design of the RCHS comprehensive program. An alternative school model, RCHS was created to develop, demonstrate, and disseminate models of identification, curriculum, governance, and program evaluation that meet the needs of gifted students from economically disadvantaged circumstances or culturally diverse backgrounds, many of whom are underachievers (Dabney, 1977). The majority of the students at RCHS are African American. Given the uniqueness of their characteristics, these gifted learners—particularly those from economically disadvantaged environments—present special challenges to teachers because they bring unique understandings, experiences, and perceptions to the classroom. The RCHS model was based on the premise that an effective schooling experience could be designed using the particular learning styles, strengths, gifts, talents, and instructional needs of African-American learners as a base.

The first class of RCHS students entered from feeder middle schools around the city of Richmond in 1977. Now, almost 20 years later, RCHS is a thriving learning community. Recognized as an exemplary program model for gifted learners from culturally diverse and low income backgrounds (Alamprese & Erlanger, 1988), RCHS boasts a unique course of study; staff who are trained to attend to students' individual needs; and graduates who are offered admission to some of the country's most prestigious colleges and universities, among them Boston University, Carnegie-Mellon University, The College of William and Mary, Duke,

Harvard, Stanford, The University of Virginia, Yale, and West Point Military Academy. Since 1986, RCHS graduates have won more than $4.8 million in grants, scholarships, and financial aid. As highlighted in the RCHS school brochure, Kappa Delta Pi listed RCHS in its *A Report of the Good School Project: One Hundred Good Schools.* Additionally, RCHS was selected by the Carnegie Foundation as one of 200 high schools in the nation promoting excellence in education (RCHS, 1991).

As with any other school, the core of Richmond Community High School's success is reflected in the classroom. Having teachers who understand the diverse learning styles and strengths of their student population is essential to the school's success. RCHS teachers acknowledge that their student population expresses giftedness in a manner that is often different from the traditional manifestations of linear, logical-sequential expressions. Thus, teachers use divergent instructional strategies to engage their students in the learning experience. Examples of these types of strategies appear below in classroom teacher Dennis Reed's description of his 10th-grade class in global literature.

FROM THE EXPERIENCE OF ONE TEACHER

Teaching African-American gifted students in this global literature class offers the opportunity to introduce them to the work of a variety of creative writers and to interact with them as they express their own responses to the world around them. Close observation of the mind set of my students reveals that they think in episodic, visual, and often poetic ways. I have taught students of varying abilities. Gifted students, however, respond quite differently to instruction than their age peers. They appear to be more capable of dealing with ambiguities, duplicities, and often contradictory expressions embedded in literature and historical events. Additionally, as African-American students, they have a unique capacity to express the duplicity of their own existence in unique and often colorful ways.

I am reminded of W. E. B. DuBois's description of the inner conflicts that he experienced as a young student struggling with life in mainstream America in the early 1900s. Dr. DuBois characterized these conflicts as his "warring souls." DuBois's statement is frequently quoted when discussing terms such as *duplicity, ambiguity,* and *cultural pluralism:* "One ever feels his 'twoness,' an American, a Negro . . . two souls, two thoughts, two unreconciled strivings, two warring ideals in one dark body, whose dogged strength alone keeps it from being torn asunder" (Boykin, 1986, p. 63). Not unlike DuBois, students in my classes have often expressed a sense of conflict between the acknowledgment of their giftedness and the challenges they face as young African Americans in contemporary society.

To build on the strengths that my students bring to the classroom, I recognize the challenges that they may face and use several key strategies to build a bridge or segue between who they are and the important content knowledge that they must acquire to be successful. A few of these strategies are:

1. Providing opportunities for oral discourse on materials read, using problem-based learning strategies as a framework for building discussions.
2. Selecting materials written by contemporary and historical writers and historians of similar ethnic, gender, and class backgrounds.
3. Selecting materials that reflect life themes that students can identify with (e.g., teenage identity dilemmas, religious and philosophical themes, intergenerational relations, intra- and intergender relations, etc.).

Selecting materials by writers such as Toni Cade Bambara, Gwendolyn Brooks, Toni Morrison, Imiri Baraka, Haki Matibuti, Allen Ginsberg, and Jack Kerouac usually works well with my students because the work of these writers is characterized by their personal narratives; colorful, descriptive writing styles; and the similarities of themes across cultural and gender groups.

In-class activities such as collaborative poetry, focused writing, directed narrative exercises, short story writing, dramatic monologues, radio plays, and other writing allows students opportunities for introspection, reflection, and response to the context of their own environment and that of others. Such activities accentuate the verbal and linguistic strengths of African-American students that I have witnessed in classrooms with students of varying abilities. These activities also provide opportunities for students to interact with others through drama and oral presentations.

While we spend a great deal of time on nontraditional forms of writing, poetry, and dramatic expression, we also discuss conventional forms of literature and dramatic and commercial writing. Students are often asked to bring in their own essays, sample journal entries, poetry, selected literature, and other art forms such as the lyrics of rap music (with certain restrictions on antisocial language). This work is then evaluated by asking questions such as the following: Is there a thesis or purpose specified by the author? Does the author provide supporting evidence for the thesis? Does the work reflect a beginning, middle, climax, and conclusion? Peer review and open discussion provide students with opportunities to learn from each other as they begin to value the varying viewpoints of their classmates.

Every effort is made to affirm familiar cultural modalities in class discussions by providing different examples to move the students through intellectual discussions, remembering always that, as episodic learners, they may often digress in discussion. Most interesting, however, is that even when they appear to be moving off the subject, they easily recall the conceptual basis of the work being studied. As we proceed through the initial activities, my students are able to elaborate and express a sense of connectedness with the artist.

Example

One class period, we began by discussing Toni Cade Bambara's short story "My Man Bovanne." To stir up conversation, I asked questions such as "What do you think of the language?" or "How about that first line, 'blind people got a hummin' jones if you notice?'" The phrase "hummin' jones" evoked a discussion of dialects, or sayings, of different cultures. The students then identified and shared other familiar sayings and metaphors. We con-

tinued by discussing Bambara's lyrical, rhythmic style of writing.

Later, one of the students pointed out how unconventional Bambara's sentences are, describing them as "not like standard English." A discussion of different writing approaches followed, with emphasis on how successful Bambara's language is at using a circular approach in its characterization and themes. Other issues such as social commentary in writing, commonalities across varying ethnic groups, dialects, censorship, parallel story themes across cultures, and marketability emerged as we read and reviewed the work of such writers as Imiri Baraka, Allen Ginsberg, Gwendolyn Brooks, and others.

Recommendations

The strategies that follow summarize some of the methodologies I use to match my students' strengths with the desired learning and thereby make the connection that is necessary for maximum learning to occur.

1. Use material that is culturally affirming, created by authors of a similar culture, gender, and class. This is important to establish a sense of identity, context, and trust in the legitimacy of the learning experience. (Lists generated by the Black Caucus of the National Council of Teachers of English are highly recommended.)
2. Select work that is expressive of a familiar paradigm (e.g., cyclical, episodic idiom in writing such as the works of Toni Morrison, Toni Cade Bambara, and John Edgar Wideman) that students may later use in their own writings.
3. Prepare instructional activities designed to develop the multiple strengths of students (e.g., creative writing, poetry, public speaking, debating, and multidisciplinary/multimedia projects).
4. Use direct instruction strategies to maximize learners' critical and creative thinking abilities. I have found teaching metacognitive thinking, teaching creative/divergent thinking, requiring use of logs and journals to document thoughts for future writing, and using call-and-response techniques to aid in

memory retention have been effective with my students.

CONCLUSION

A teacher's sensitivity to the manner in which students receive, process, and respond to instruction is critical to connecting with them in a positive way in the classroom. While the mechanics of English and the study of the various idioms of literature are imbedded in good teaching, equally important is the teacher's understanding the context of students' backgrounds, the experiences that they bring to class daily, their strengths, and their preferred modes of learning.

Creating instructional experiences that students can relate to provides substance and mean-ing to learning that has a long-term impact. Through these substantive learning experiences, their gifts and talents are maximized.

As long as traditional instructional methodologies continue to be held as the standard by which all students are measured, without specific attention to the strengths and needs of individual students and the cultural bases from which they originate, what we do in the name of schooling may continue to miss the mark. We can no longer afford to allow the valuable gifts and talents of African Americans or those of any other students from culturally diverse backgrounds to go undeveloped. Utilizing instructional methodologies that connect the learner with the desired learning experience will go far toward nurturing the unique traits of all gifted students and move us more swiftly toward designing a positive future for them.

REFERENCES

Alamprese, J. A., & Erlanger, W. J. (1988). No gift wasted. *Effective strategies for educating highly able, disadvantaged students in mathematics and science, Vol. 1: Findings.* Washington, DC: Cosmos.

Baldwin, A. Y. (1989). The purpose of education for gifted Black students. In C. J. Maker (Ed.), *Critical issues in gifted education: Vol. 2: Defensible programs for cultural and ethnic minorities.* (pp. 237–245). Austin, TX: Pro-Ed.

Boykin, A. W. (1986). The triple quandary and the schooling of Afro-American children. In U. Neisser (Ed.), *The school achievement of minority children.* (pp. 57–92). Hillsdale, NJ: Erlbaum.

Clark, B. (1988). *Growing up gifted* (3rd ed.). Columbus, OH: Merrill.

Dabney, M. G. (1977). Report of an experiment: Gifted education at Richmond Community High School. *The Secondary School Experiential Learning Community Project.* Richmond: Richmond Public Schools and Virginia State University.

Ford, D. Y., & Harris, J. J. III. (1991). On discovering the hidden treasure of gifted and talented African-American children. *Roeper Review, 13* (1), 27–33.

Fordham, S., & Ogbu, J. (1986). Black students' school success: Coping with the burden of acting white. *The Urban Review, 8,* 176–206.

Frasier, M. M. (1989). Identification of gifted Black students: Developing new perspectives. In C. J. Maker & S. W. Schiever (Eds.), *Critical issues in gifted education: Vol. 2. Defensible programs for cultural and ethnic minorities* (pp.213–225). Austin, TX: Pro-Ed.

Gallagher, J. J. (1995). Education of gifted students: A civil rights issue? *Phi Delta Kappan,* 408–410.

Hale-Benson, J. (1986). *Black children: Their roots, culture and learning styles.* Baltimore: John Hopkins University Press.

Hilliard, A. (1976). *Alternative to IQ testing: An approach to the identification of the gifted in minority children* (Report No. 75175). San Francisco: San Francisco State University.

Patton, J. M., & Baytops, J. L. (1995). Identifying and transforming the potential of young, gifted African Americans: A clarion call for action. In B. A. Ford, F. E. Obiakor, & J. M. Patton (Eds.), *Effective education for African-American exceptional learners: New perspectives.* (pp. 27–67). Austin, TX: ProEd.

Peterson, N. L. (1996). The role of responsive classrooms in respecting and infusing cultural diversity in gifted education. Unpublished manuscript. Charlottesville, VA: National Association for Gifted Children, Task Force on Diversity.

Shade, B. (1990). *Engaging the battle for African-American minds.* (Commissioned paper). Dallas, TX: National Alliance for Black School Educators.

United States Department of Education. (1995). *National excellence: A case for developing America's talent.* Washington, DC: Office of Educational Research and Improvement.

ABOUT THE AUTHORS

JOY L. BAYTOPS, Specialist, Programs for the Gifted, Virginia Department of Education, Richmond, Virginia. DENNIS REED, Writing Instructor, Richmond Community High School, Richmond, Virginia.

IN THE ORAL TRADITION

*This section of **Multiple Voices** capitalizes on the oral tradition common to many cultures. In this tradition, history and cultural values are transmitted from one generation to another by word of mouth. In some cultures, a specific person carries the responsibility of learning the stories of the people and telling them on demand and at appropriate events to inform and guide the people. Some American Indians refer to the stories as the "library" of their people.*

"In the Oral Tradition" presents interviews with eminent scholars and community leaders in the education and service of exceptional learners from culturally and linguistically diverse backgrounds. These "elders" of the education community share their perspectives and prognostications on pertinent issues.

Understanding and Serving American Indian Children with Special Needs

HELEN BESSENT BYRD, PROFESSOR
Norfolk State University

Helen Bessent Byrd, Professor, Special Education Department, Norfolk State University, Norfolk, Virginia, the feature editor, conducted the interviews. The interviewees are Martha Gorospe, Director of the EPICS Project (a federally funded national parent training, information, and technical assistance center), Bernalillo, New Mexico; Leon A. Nuvayestewa, Sr., Manager of Human Services, The Hopi Tribe, Kykotsmovi, Arizona; and Evelyn Klimpel, Multicultural Programs Coordinator, North Dakota Center for Persons with Disabilities, Minot State University, Minot, North Dakota.

Klimpel: As we begin, I would like to humble myself before my elders and tribal members as I speak about these different topics. I would like to ask them for forgiveness in case I make a mistake. This is a tradition, that we pay respect to our elders before we speak.

Byrd: Thank you all for sharing your thoughts on this important topic. Like other groups in our society today, there is some equivocation regarding the name by which your people are called. For us African Americans, as an example, there is a choice of African American or Black American. Do

you prefer to be referred to as American Indian, Native American, or by some other name? Please indicate whether there is some general consensus or any politically correct term.

Nuvayestewa: You are correct that people have used different names to identify specific populations and groups. I think the politically correct name they are using right now is *Native American.* It seems that the consensus, at least with the Arizona tribes, is that Native American is the name that has been accepted. Specifically within my tribe, the Hopi, we will continue to call ourselves the Hopi people. On the logo of our stationary for the tribal offices, it says the "The Hopi Tribe." That is really our preference, and we have always used it, while the other agencies still continue to refer to us as a group of people called *Native American.* That has been the consensus for tribes in Arizona.

Gorospe: I feel the need to explain why I would decide to be called an American Indian versus what I would feel more comfortable with in my own community. In the past I have experienced some sarcasm along the way. It has occurred often enough for me to form my own opinion as to how I would like to be addressed as an ethnic person. And that would be to be called an American Indian. With the term *Indian population,* I have met people who confused American Indians with East Indians. And because I am dark skinned, it creates some confusion. In our own Indian communities (not just in New Mexico, but in other tribal communities around the country) Indian people do not refer to each other as Native Americans or American Indians. Generally we ask, "What kind of Indian are you?" or "Where are you from?" If I say that I am from the Southwest, they would respond by asking whether I am Apache, Navaho, or Pueblo. If I am from South Dakota, they might ask whether I am Sioux, or if I am from California, Pomo.

If you want to think in terms of what is politically correct, consider the names of the organizations that have impacted this entire country for American Indians in some form or another. Examples are the American Indian Movement and the American Indian Congress. There is another term coming into use, *First*

Nation. I think that it adds to the confusion, although it makes sense to me because we were already here as individual nations or tribal groups when European contact occurred. That would be my next preference. Although *American Indian* sounds good to me, there is a lot of controversy over Columbus discovering America. That was incorrect from the beginning.

Klimpel: What I have found is that it is a personal preference. It is true that every so often you will hear the most politically correct term, and the last one I heard was that you should be called by your tribal affiliation. In any case, if they asked me what I wanted to be called I would say *Crow/Hidatso Indian.* However, the most popular term that I hear is *American Indian.*

Byrd: For the purposes of this article we will use the term *American Indian.* Now please address how life experiences that are unique to them impact the parental involvement of American Indian people in the education of their children.

Klimpel: I believe that historically education has scared Indian people because their children were taken away from them to boarding schools. They were taught the dominant society's culture and taught not to practice or learn about their own culture. And of course our own culture is very important to us, so it is a trust issue. Indian people are fearful of education. If students are educated, it is feared, they will forget who they are—a matter that is very important to native people. Many parents are a little hesitant to become involved with educators. They need to gain trust from these parents and let them know that they are looking out for the child's best interest.

Gorospe: There are several things unique to Indian people. I will choose to speak basically from my own community and the communities in which I have worked. I certainly cannot speak for all; however, I do know that the southwest and other parts of the country had the boarding school era when children were taken away from their families to attend residential schools. This occurred because either they were from very rural environments or they did not have schools in their communities. So, they recruited these children and had them attend [schools outside the community]. Some of these schools were Bureau of Indian Affairs (BIA), U. S. Department of Interior schools, which were basically academic as well as addressing other needs that were felt at the time to be important for American Indians to more effectively assimilate into the mainstream. This era took away the culture of these students. Some of them lost their way. I think that the impact of schools that were of a religious nature, such as Mormon, Baptist, and Methodist, redirected the students in relationship to the American Indian culture. Regarding the Bureau schools, there have been several studies, and one in particular by an Indian man who is a professor at the University of New Mexico. He has stated that here in New Mexico many of the Indians who did go to boarding school did not go very far away, but far enough away to be removed from their immediate family members. These individuals returned to the blanket (an Indian expression) so that they could maintain and keep the culture going. I think that with these families they found a balance between the two cultures.

Sometimes I think that families that do not live on the reservation but live in the urban areas are not as culturally grounded as those who live on the reservation. In my experience and those of my Indian friends, we have found it necessary to go back and forth to maintain our culture and our religion. Growing up as Indian people, we are taught not to ask too many questions and not to question authority. Life and age experiences traditionally were much more important than educational background for a younger person versus an older person. Because of that, taking children away to boarding school had an impact on the involvement that parents had with their children's educational program. Whether the child had a disability or not, it was something that was not experienced. If children were taken away to school at 5 years of age, they were without their own ethnic role models for their educational program. Because the boarding schools are not as prominent any more, change is coming about for families who are becoming more involved.

It is important for the American Indian families to become knowledgeable about how to be more actively involved. They require skills to do that. Communication skills are needed. If they are not accustomed to dealing with non-Indian people, they may find it difficult to talk about some of the things they would like their children to experience in education. When we engage in our cultural activities, it is very sacred to us. It is very difficult to talk about the cultural things that we do. Among the Pueblo people, it is an unspoken rule that families do not divulge information pertaining to their religion. We have done a lot of training on cultural sensitivity for non Indians who do not have a lot of experience working with Indian people.

In the medical field, they are surprised to find that they are often the second opinion. Many Indian families have already taken their children to Indian healers. The other difference that pertains to the medical issue is that we have always viewed things quite differently. In recent times you hear a lot about home-based or holistic approaches to medical care. We, as Indian people, have always thought of the physical, psychological, and spiritual components of humans as one. When we seek assistance from our cultural healers, it is understood that these components are intertwined with one another. It is different for us when we look at the western medical component which is fragmented and departmentalized.

I find myself as an assertive, outgoing person having to switch roles when I go back home. I need to be able to follow the rules at home as well as come out here and speak openly. I have not always been that way. In my personal experience, I have a child who was medically impaired early on, and I used a wonderful pediatrician who did wonderful things for us. However, my son's prognosis was not very good. But then he began to get better and better. The doctor had no explanation for us. I had one for the pediatrician, but I did not share it with him because I was not comfortable sharing that part of our culture and our life with him. Many Indian parents are not comfortable sharing information like that. When I have shared that information in my professional experience I get responses like, "Well, this is wonderful. We could save lots of children"; "We could make some big differences if we could just utilize what you have utilized with your child." My response has been, "No." This is something that you can't just do. This is a way of life. It is a life-long experience. It is a belief system within one's own being that helps these things come about.

Nuvayestewa: There have been unique differences traditionally and throughout the years that our tribe has been impacted by the outside. (We refer to the "outside" as anything that is off the reservation. This would be the outside dominant society.) We are a minority, and I think that has had a major impact on how families and the vast experience have begun to change. Traditionally, I am talking about how the Hopi tribe and the Hopi family were dealing with special needs of children before the dominant society began to categorize people and their needs. That wasn't something that originally was an acceptable thing within the tribe. What happened was the family, the individual in that family, the community, and the village were cognizant of the people with special needs, but they did not categorize them. They were always a part of, never outside of, the larger group. As a result, any experiences that came out of their being a part of the group were always just the way the things were. So when the child went to the school setting, hopefully what was being practiced in the community also was being transferred into the schools. And so, special needs children at a lot of schools on the reservation were essentially supported by the learning that was happening with all of the other individuals. Therefore, there was no special attention, *per se,* given to those individuals with special needs. They were kind of mainstreamed.

Later on, as the dominant society began to categorize people, we began to separate the exceptional child who had special needs. Then resources for that individual were secured to provide that support. In a way, there was a positive impact because individuals were identified as having special needs, and then the resources came to those individuals to help them. This also began to have a negative impact, because now you were categorizing people, which was not in the true sense of community. Now you were identifying people as special or having a special need, which was not

traditionally the correct way to do it from the Hopi perspective. But we had to deal with that in some way, so the life experiences provided by the parents and then from the individual's going to the school system were really valuable. The parent was providing support, so I think it is no different today from what you see in the dominant society. It's just that what happened was that by categorizing people and providing specific resources for the child you got into this mode of institutionalizing people. So the special needs child began to get tied into a special program and eventually placed in a special institution. For our people, having special needs meant locating that person off the reservation and into an institution. I think that the experiences that we have here, at least regarding parental involvement, were and still are very positive.

There are special kinds of skills required to provide support to the special needs child. The parents had to learn those special skills and different ways of dealing with the special needs. Some parents probably had difficulty in providing that support because they didn't have the skills initially and had to learn them. There have been some instances when the parents had to follow the child to the institution or find employment within the vicinity of the institution where the child was located, so they did that to be close to their child. This tells me that the parents have always continued to provide support. An important factor in the relocation of the special needs child and parents is the cultural side of the life experience. There is a lot of history and knowledge that is transferred orally to children within the home. An example is language. The first language that students should normally learn is their own language, which is Hopi. Then they learn the dominant society's language, which is English. So, once you have relocated that special needs child at an institution that is off the reservation or in another state, then that connection is broken. The parents, knowing that happens, try to provide the oral knowledge by being there with the child if they can. If they can't be present, they try to find another way to provide that cultural information to the child. We would prefer, at this point, to have those services available right here in the schools that we have. So that is our major goal. We are getting there, but it is very slow, as you know, because resources are not always available.

Byrd: To what extent do cultural beliefs and practices of American Indian people impede or enhance their participation in policymaking and service utilization by their children who are exceptional learners?

Gorospe: We have always done a lot of training for Indian parents of children with disabilities. There are some who become very assertive and very interactive. They feel comfortable informing the educators of what they would like to see or affirming what their child is doing in the program that will help enhance the child's education. Taking it a step further, some parents assume the role of getting other parents to participate and offer their expertise for systems advocacy. Rarely will you find Indian people on steering committees or task forces. I think a lot of parents need positive affirmation to do that. We need some guidelines to help us be effective on boards once you identify Indian families that want to get involved. Agencies should strongly connect with these individuals and continue to be supportive. Families may speak English, but they may be more comfortable hearing this vital information about their child in their Indian language. It is important to address that issue by having an interpreter's assistance. There are some provisions under special education law that make it mandatory, but that does not always happen. The language can be a very difficult barrier.

Nuvayestewa: Consistent with the Hopi cultural beliefs and practices, there has always been a positive participation by our people in making policy and having the people utilize the services that are available. There is a requirement from the tribe and the elders that has always promoted self-sufficiency. They have always encouraged our people to work out things on their own. We don't want to become a dependent state, or a tribe dependent on any services. The direction has been, so far, to utilize the services but be cognizant that we have to do on our own as well. This has to be balanced out, not to be totally dependent. So the parent has to make that decision.

I think that parents have decided to have other institutions provide assistance to their special needs children to some extent without being totally dependent. This requires the parents to become knowledgeable in that area so they will have the skills to fill that gap in providing support. That is where we have been having major difficulty on our reservation because we are isolated. What we are planning to do is make interactive television available throughout the reservation to provide training and consultation to parents who need it. We have it available at one of our high schools right now. But we want it available to the whole community. This would be in line with capacity building—building the capacity of the individual, the family, and the village to take care of their own. That is what we would like to see. Because we are in an isolated area, there are limited provider agencies on our reservations now. However, if you need services on a multiple level, then you must go to the nearest town, which is 92 miles away. So the way to address the problems of children with special needs is to use that interactive television, use the consultation, and get the training to the parents. Parents are directly involved as a matter of fact. That occurs not only in the Individuals with Disabilities Education Act (IDEA) program, but also in Head Start. The parents are there deciding what is needed for the child. We make sure that the parents are there and in agreement with what is being recommended. And, of course, we still have our Hopi ceremonial cycle, and it really is the religious activities of the tribe. So the school system does schedule around that as much as possible. I am not aware that these cultural practices are a big problem.

Kimpel: You could wrap it up in one word—our *spirituality*. Our cultural beliefs and practices all are one. So, if a service agency or school system does not understand the individual spirituality of the family, it does not understand the background, and that could impede the services. It is very important that the service providers understand the culture of the tribe with which they are working. If they do understand the tribe they are working with, it really enhances parent participation. It helps if the parents see those teachers participating at their cultural events, feel that they are welcomed into the school by the teachers, and sense that the tribal culture is integrated into the curriculum. You will see a lot of parent participation and a lot of support.

The feeling of freedom to be involved in policymaking is getting better. What we have found is that we need education to better ourselves, our families, and our tribes. By doing that we now have more educated tribal members who are getting into positions of policymaking and having input. This is better for everyone.

Byrd: What nuances are there, if any, with regard to the matter of sovereignty for Indian people and compliance with federal laws regarding people with disabilities?

Nuvayestewa: The Hopi tribal council is the governing body for the people. They are aware of the federal laws, and they approve these programs that are coming in, like the IDEA program, et cetera. And they are required to comply with federal laws. The members of the tribal council are also aware that they have to exercise their sovereignty. Therefore, on any compliance requirements they are attentive to the laws that have been passed, especially federal laws.

The tribal council wants to be more aware of some of these laws, because some of the laws do not fit the Hopi people the way they want them to fit. There are negative impacts from some of the federal laws that have been posted. The Hopi people want to be more specific about how these laws would be accepted on the reservation rather than not comply with them. That means that they would modify the sections of the law that were not fitting the needs of the people and revise it in such a way that it really provides a positive support for a way of life.

In IDEA and in the Americans with Disabilities Act programs, there are certain sections that need to be changed. The law requires you have to have certain things such as accessibility to buildings. Those requirements are not a problem. The problems arise when the law requires other things that are not possible on a reservation. An example is automatic doors. These are costly items that are not needed in our public facilities. Another example is sidewalks. If you come to our reservation you are not going to see sidewalks. But under the law, you need to provide some means of accessibility by having sidewalks. Another example is the setting for elderly care. Our elderly are more than willing to be housed in facilities that do not meet all the federal requirements for a nursing home. They don't need all this lighting we are used to having. They may be comfortable with a lantern. Our elderly are more comfortable in their home setting where they have spiritual and social connections. They prefer the relationships with family and community. So that is more specific to their needs, and that is what they want. If it satisfies them to have a lantern, then why can't we provide them with a lantern rather than having these modern lights? It is really not trying to satisfy their needs, but being in compliance with the law. All of our roads, incidentally, are not paved either. We have dirt roads. So when we have inclement weather, it is very muddy out there. Those are just some examples. Material things are not their primary concern. So we would like to have the flexibility to modify the regulations for expenditures. The family and its bonding are more important than what the regulations mandate.

Kimpel: The sovereignty of our Indian people sometimes is used for positive things and sometimes for negative things. Sometimes, federal and state laws will use the sovereignty issue as a way to avoid servicing people with disabilities on the reservation. Or, because of the sovereignty issue, we are assisted by the BIA and are involved in two tracking systems. Then sometimes when special needs students move off the reservation they get lost in the shuffle. Also, regarding the funding for students with disabilities, when they are not counted there is less funding, because one child is counted under BIA but not counted under the state system. What we have been wanting on our reservations in North Dakota is our own special education units. Two of our reservations do have one that is working out very well. They are able to keep track of their students and make sure the services are being implemented. However, one of our reservations is serviced in five different districts, so a student may move 20 miles away and be in a different unit and the paperwork does not always follow him or her. We want the reservation to have its own special education unit so that it can keep track of all the students. Also, personnel could make sure that the individualized education programs are following the students and that the plans are being implemented. Well, we do have four reservations, and two of them do have their own units, which is wonderful. We are still pushing for the other two reservations!

Gorospe: Because of our sovereignty many of the Indian tribes throughout the country have not had a strong relationship with their state leadership or state government. Basically this is because there are many tribes that have received funding from BIA to set up programs such as social services, although BIA does not have as many services as the state might. State interaction with Indian programs may not exist. When Indian people travel long distances to utilize services, it makes it very inconvenient for families. That has always been an issue. Sovereignty for our people has been a real stronghold. It has allowed us to govern ourselves in a way that we see appropriate for Indian people. When we have political issues going on, it is not usual to have tribal members keeping an ear open for information regarding how their tribal leadership is going to endorse or not endorse that issue. There have been situations for Pueblo people where they used an outside school for the younger children for whom the school was not addressing some educational issues for the Indian children. The governor of the Pueblo said, "We have a school within the village. Our children will not attend your school."

There is a gang situation throughout the country. One example of how strongly the tribal government leadership is entwined with the religion occurred in one of our very small traditional villages. When some gang issues became prevalent, the Indian leadership said, "What the gangs are doing is not appropriate for us here. We have never had this kind of conflict. We don't like the outcome of it, and we don't care too much for your presence. You need to give your children an option, and if they don't want to follow the rules of the village, then they will have to pack up and leave. They can go to the nearby cities that have

gangs if that is what they want. It is interesting. It is a lecture versus a ruling that happened. The children just said "It is over," and their native beliefs took priority. I don't frequently discuss the gambling issue, but that and sovereignty have a lot to do with how the Indian people throughout the country who have gaming industries have managed to find resources to better their communities. Some of these resources have ranged from educational to housing, recreational, and emergency services. This has made a big difference in the community. However, the gaming industry is still very controversial.

Byrd: Please cite any strategies in the delivery of services to American Indian exceptional learners that are successful today or portend to be successful in the future.

Nuvayestewa: I think one of them that I talked about was interactive television and the idea of getting consultation to the local level of the village and to the families that need that help. Also, interactive television could be used for educational programs to provide skills to families and other individuals to take care of the special needs population. I know that when I went to Washington to meet with Commissioner Williams I saw how technology was being used by him. Not a lot of that technology is readily available here on our reservation. There are great possibilities with our special needs children, but we have not fully tapped that potential yet. There are some other strategies that we have used or can use. We worked with the National Foundation for the Blind from New York and developed cassette tapes on how to bake bread and prepare traditional meals for individuals who are blind. We have used these cassettes with individuals who are visually impaired. That can also work for exceptional children, if we can redesign the program in such a way that they are able to use that type of technology. Seeing the possible uses of technology shows that we have grossly underutilized the talents of special needs children. We've categorized and put limits on them.

Gorospe: There is a disproportionately large number of American Indian students in special education throughout the country. This may be due to the use of standardized tests developed in the mainstream for testing American Indian children. The assessment of Indian children should be done in such a way as to enhance their ability to express their own individuality and their intelligence as well as academics within their culture.

Language is a big barrier when it comes to evaluating our children. Many of our children are labeled as learning disabled or speech impaired. An Indian language may be the child's first language. It is different from that of any other ethnic group, because the Indian language is not written for a lot of our tribes. We here at EPICS do a lot of role playing and examples. In the Pueblos, we have huge outdoor ovens that we bake our bread in. These ovens have no temperature gauges. They are just big and round. We learn to bake from experience passed down for generations. This is a very productive way for Indian children to learn.

Indian families need skills to communicate more effectively. Families also need skills in conflict resolution. They need to be taught that they can disagree, that disagreement brings about creative changes for the better. It is okay to become emotional, but learn to ask for breaks when you do that. They need skills to ask for clarification to understand different concepts. Lots of families, when they don't understand, will agree with something and go away without fully comprehending. Indian people relied on trusting the people disseminating information or training. There are a lot of skills that parents need to facilitate their children's educational progress.

Kimpel: Yes, what we need, of course, is to get more Indian educators out there, and that is the big push. Our tribal colleges are doing a wonderful job of getting that started, and now we need to get into the special education aspect. That is new to our tribal colleges, but they have been developing that aspect for the past 2 years. I think that it is wonderful to do it, because Indian students want to feel comfortable when they are in a classroom. They want to see someone like themselves. Also, the students enjoy seeing their teachers at the pow wow dancing with the native people, enjoying

themselves, knowing the language. All of these factors make students comfortable in the environment of the classroom. Then they're ready to learn, to respect that teacher, and to trust that teacher. Like I said earlier, trust is an important issue in the entire process. The students need to understand what the teacher's motives are and that the teacher's goal is to make each student the best that he or she can be. Also, the teacher needs to understand the culture of the community in which he or she is working. It is very important not only to understand the environment but also to participate in it, socializing with the people after school hours. Indian people are very social people, and that is important to us. If you are going to be friendly with me at school or at your business, I expect the same after hours too.

Byrd: Are there any other points that you would like to make at this time?

Kimpel: Understanding tribal government is very important. If the professionals understand the tribal policies and how those policies affect their students and families, these personnel can deliver appropriate services. If they can get the state agencies and tribal agencies to collaborate and work together with no hidden agendas on either side, we can do our children justice.

Gorospe: Training on a culturally sensitive approach to Indian communities is helpful if people are working with Indian groups and are not very familiar with them. There are wonderful ways to approach the community and become respected and invited into the Indian community. People who have worked in the Indian communities have maintained their relationships with Indian people. That can happen if the community is approached in a sensitive way.

Nuvayestewa: What we have been promoting is the special needs parent group. There is a potential for an individual to achieve at any level we want him or her to achieve. We as parents have always put limits on children, saying, "They're not able to do this so I am not going to expect any more than that." This type of thinking has got to change. I think that we have begun to change that attitude because we found in our experience that the potential for great achievement is there.

We need to provide from within our own communities the resources for the children to excel, and the way to do that is through education, providing the skills to the parents and building the capacity right in the family. Developmental disabilities specialists are here for a while and then they leave. We are in a rural, isolated area, and we don't have all the specialists we need to have here on the reservation. Therefore, we have to build that knowledge within the community. You educate the individual, empower the family and community, and build the capacity into the community. We have made our people dependent on a system of care. That should not continue. Now we need to reverse that. The people can do it. I think the special child has all the potential to excel in any area, and we need to provide the opportunity.

I have been with these programs for a long time, so I understand them a little. Much of my understanding comes from the elderly people, so I appreciate them.

Byrd: Thanks so much to each of you. You have improved understanding of the context and services to American Indian children with special needs and their families. Indeed, you have passed on wisdom from your elders and knowledge from your experiences. This is an invaluable contribution to the education of American Indian children.

ABOUT THE AUTHORS

HELEN BESSENT BYRD, Professor, Norfolk State University.